CRUISING THE MEDITERRANEAN

CRUISING THE MEDITERRANEAN

A TRAVEL MEMOIR

Al & Sunny Lockwood

Front Porch Publishing
Hendersonville, N. C.

ISBN: 069259986X
ISBN 13: 9780692599860

Cover design by Parker Wallman
www.wallmandesign.com

Other travel memoirs by Al & Sunny Lockwood

Finding Ourselves in Venice, Florence, Rome & Barcelona

Cruising the Atlantic

Cruising Panama's Canal

TABLE OF CONTENTS

MAY WE INTRODUCE OURSELVES

Al and I met rather late in life, long after college and careers. We met at a writer's conference in the tiny village of Volcano in Amador County, California.

Volcano is one of the Gold Rush towns scattered among the western foothills and mountain slopes of the Sierra Nevada along a five-county region known as California's Mother Lode.

I had recently moved to Calaveras County (a neighboring Mother Lode county), bought a monthly community newspaper with two partners and was attending the conference in hopes of meeting writers who might contribute to our publication, or who might become friends in my new home.

Although I'd been coming to Calaveras for years as a weekend escape from the stress and pressure of the San Francisco Bay Area, I knew few locals well and hoped this conference would change that.

At the Saturday night conference banquet, Al Lockwood and I sat at the same table along with three others. Each of us at the table introduced ourselves and told a little about our writing.

Although I'd heard Al read one of his stories earlier in the day and had been moved to both tears and laughter by his prose, when he introduced himself he talked about his photography. He said he was specializing in wildflowers of the mid-Sierra and had work hanging in local galleries.

I was so excited to meet someone who knew about the local plant life that I nearly monopolized him all evening, asking about trees and flowers and grasses of the area. I had been trying for years to find someone who could tell me about local plants, and here was a wildflower photographer sitting at my table. He volunteered to take me out on a shoot.

Turns out, he was as interested in my monthly newspaper as I was in his wildflower photography. He'd been looking for a chance to join a newspaper staff as a photo editor. Since my partners and I had no photo editor, we agreed to bring him onboard. He was far more tech-savvy than we were and helped develop our paper in a number of ways.

His photography was even better than his writing, and soon he was not only working with photos others brought to the paper, he was also writing a regular wildflower column, complete with stunning images and witty copy.

True to his word, he took me on more than one photo shoot. As he drove me along potholed logging roads in his blue Ford-150, or as we hiked rocky mountain paths, he pointed out the various wildflowers, explaining how to identify them.

From elegant brodiaea nodding in the breeze on low-elevation hillsides, to cliffside fairy lanterns and ground-hugging pussy paws, he delighted in showing me the flora of the region. And I was able to observe his gentle spirit as he photographed flowers and ferns, mosses and mushrooms.

As we became better acquainted, I was amazed at all we shared in common. We had both graduated from San Jose State University – he with a degree in engineering, I with a degree in writing. He had a master's of divinity from Golden Gate Baptist Theological Seminary. I had a master's of spirituality from Santa Clara University. Although we'd both been married and divorced, neither of us had children. We both love nature and art and photography and books and travel.

It wasn't long for feelings of friendship to grow into something more.

✲✲

That all happened in 1999.

Today, Al and I have retired from full-time employment.

Because of declining health, we moved across California from the Gold Rush foothills of Calaveras County where Mark Twain searched for nuggets and wrote short stories, to coastal Sonoma County where Jack London farmed and wrote.

Although the years rush past with ever-increasing speed, we continue to pursue our creative interests (Al with his camera, I with my notebook and pen), and we're either planning our next trip, or we're on it.

Come along with us on our wish-list journey and see if it doesn't spark a little wanderlust in your own heart.

DON'T LET AGING STOP YOU FROM HAVING FUN

It wasn't that long ago I went to bed at age 45 and woke up the next morning at age 65 to discover I was suddenly a "senior." What a shock! How did I get here so quickly?

I mean, I don't feel old. And, on good days, I don't think I look old either. (Of course that could be credited in part to my fading eyesight.)

Some people waking up to the reality of old age may wonder if the good times are over.

It only takes standing in line at the pharmacy for 20 minutes or languishing for hours at the doctor's office to convince us that our age has slammed the door on having fun.

But that doesn't have to be the case.

Al and I have found a couple of ways to live the good life in our "senior" years. One is serving others (volunteering, helping, mentoring, listening to those who need to share and sharing what we can of our means and ourselves).

The other is making some of our dreams come true.

Yes, making dreams come true brings wonder, excitement, fulfillment and joy. This book is about a dream-come-true journey made possible by an 86,700-ton cruise ship and our love of travel.

In 2012, a texting driver slammed into us while we were sitting at a red light. This careless driver crashed into us at 60 miles per hour, totaling our car and ruining our summer. But the wreck made us realize how fragile life is. How quickly it can be snatched away.

That's when we decided to start doing things we'd always dreamed of doing someday in the future. The top of Al's bucket list was a cruise through the Panama Canal. We took that trip, and it was so amazing that we wrote a book about it: **Cruising Panama's Canal**, *Savoring 5,000 Nautical Miles and 500,000 Decadent Calories*.

While on that cruise, Al asked my number one bucket list destination and I answered without hesitation: Venice.

I first visited Venice in the 1970s as a single woman out on my own. I was there only long enough to see St. Mark's Square with its basilica and bell tower. Yet Venice's glimmering other-worldliness lodged permanently within my heart — its shimmering beauty, its domes and spires, its tangle of buildings and lacework of canals.

In 1990, I visited Venice again: "the city of mirrors, the city of mirages, at once solid and liquid, at once air and stone," as Erica Jong writes.

On that visit I had the time to wander alleys, pause in neighborhood squares and spend a whole afternoon watching laundry dry on lines stretched between third-story windows in crumbling stone apartment houses.

But my most powerful memory of the 1990 visit was of St. Mark's Square after dark.

The square, which isn't really a square at all (it's a trapezoid), is Venice's largest public space. Colonnades line three sides of the space, and near the fourth and open side stands St. Mark's Basilica.

After sunset, lights set the square aglow. The restaurants and bars beneath its colonnaded porticoes hire bands to play after dark. On small stages set up in the square, surrounded by white linen-covered tables, the musicians play classical music and Broadway hits. And when one group finishes a set, the band members on the other side of the square start theirs.

Tourists dance to the music.

Those who take a table pay handsomely for the privilege.

But there's no penalty for standing and listening, moving from one orchestra/band stage to another as the nighttime breeze lulls with its gentle touch.

Venice is exquisite. Returning to it has always been a dream of mine.

So while we were still on the Panama Canal cruise, Sweetheart Al signed us up for a 12-day cruise beginning and ending in Venice.

He'd never been to Italy, and we didn't have the money for such a trip when he registered us. But we accumulated it. And in 2014 we were able to set off on our Mediterranean cruise.

Between 2012, when we signed on for the cruise, and 2014, when we took it, we went through a lot. Among our experiences: Al had his third heart attack. I broke my foot in a fall and discovered I have extreme osteoporosis. (Yes, I know that one sign of old age is the constant talk about personal medical conditions.)

We also sold our dream home in Angels Camp, California. Al had designed and built our Victorian-style farmhouse, standing on 22 wild acres in the Gold Rush foothills of the Sierra Nevada. We treasured that home and all the memories we made there. But his health demanded we move closer to doctors and specialized medical centers.

The move also required that we sell or give away almost everything we owned within the house, the garage, my writer's cottage and Al's studio. We had to reduce our load because our retirement cottage is only 1,000 square feet. And has no garage.

So in addition to selling our Angels Camp property, we also shed most of our furniture, rugs, draperies, dishes, artworks, clothing and tons of books, records and other things.

The experience was emotional and difficult. And because we sold during the Great Recession, our real estate "nest egg" shrank dramatically from what we envisioned as an ostrich egg to about the size of a robin's egg. Nonetheless, we knew that with careful planning, we could take a Mediterranean cruise.

Because we could do it, even with our age, medical conditions and much-reduced travel funds, we think others can also enjoy their wish list travels. It just takes planning and a little imagination.

WHY WE LOVE CRUISING

Al and I enjoy road trips and weekend getaways. But ocean cruising has become our favorite long-distance form of travel. Here's why:

Value. The price of a cruise includes transportation, lodging, all the meals and snacks we desire, entertainment from movies to Broadway-style musicals and other live performances and an array of onboard and off-ship activities.

Depending on our room choice, we can be as be as thrifty or extravagant as we wish. Prices for our 12-day Mediterranean cruise ranged from $999 per person for a double-occupancy inside cabin to well over $5,000 per person for a suite.

Convenience. We unpack once. Someone else does all the "driving." We never have to check a map or double-check a GPS. We're just along for a lovely ride.

Comfort. Cruise lines aim to pamper. No matter the cost of a stateroom – from suites to inside cabins – we'll find luxurious bedding, fluffy towels and wash cloths and very nice soaps and shampoos. Some lines include body lotions, cotton balls and (on your pillow each evening) a little foil-wrapped chocolate.

Social life. Cruising offers opportunities to meet others who share our interests. Sharing travel experiences can form the basis of lifelong friendships.

Togetherness. There's nothing like carefree travel together to renew or deepen romance. Cruising is the "together travel" style for making great memories without a lot of stress.

Ease for aching bones and joints. At our age, with limited mobility and diminishing energy, knowing our cabin is nearby is most reassuring. If our knees give out or our energy lags, we can simply go to our cabin (our little home at sea) and take a nap. Or we can ease into a chair in the library and read a book. Or we can ease into a deck lounge and simply watch the sea go by.

We don't have to climb stairs, since cruise ships have elevators, and if our knees or hips give out completely we can most likely rent a scooter or wheelchair and continue to get around onboard.

Medical help nearby. The cruise ship has a doctor on board. We find that reassuring.

Destinations. Cruises take us places we're unlikely to visit on our own.

This Oct. 3 to 15 cruise will stop at Athens, Santorini, Lesbos and Argostoli, Greece; Istanbul and Ephesus, Turkey; as well as Venice. So we'll see seven different cities, world-class and historic. Now that's exciting!

PLANNING OUR TRIP

We'd been talking about our Mediterranean cruise for two years. And by April 2014, I began worrying about it. Now the nice thing about cruises is that there's nothing to worry about. You choose your stateroom and dinner arrangements, board the ship and everything's taken care of – lodging, meals, transportation, entertainment – all you have to do is enjoy.

But, I began to worry.

In the "old days," as we now refer to our youth, I'd just toss a few things in a suitcase, buy a plane ticket and take off. As I tried to recall my past European forays, I couldn't even remember how I first got to Venice.

Oh, I remember arriving, stepping down from the train and walking over to the canal and seeing those terra-cotta buildings shimmering in the choppy, pale green water, and the water reflecting off the buildings in bright shining waves. It was like nothing I'd ever seen. It was like landing on a planet too beautiful for words. The enchantment of that first impression has never left me.

As I imagined being there again, and the fun of introducing Al to St. Mark's Square, I worried about jet lag. In the "old days" the inner fog of jet lag never stopped me. But now, I imagined that we'd need at least a couple of days to recover from the long flight and the many time zone changes.

Every morning at breakfast, I'd mention my concern. Al would glance up from the newspaper and nod. Finally, one morning, I said, "I don't want to start my bucket list cruise in a fog. I want to be sharp and awake and aware from the moment we step on board. So I think we need to fly over there a few days early and work through the jet lag stuff before we start the cruise."

Suddenly Al looked interested. "Great idea," he said. "I've always wanted to go back to Amsterdam. Why don't we fly there a few days early and get acclimated? And I can have fun showing you the canals and the flower market."

Sounded good to me. I'd never been to Amsterdam, and I love new adventures. I started researching lodging in the Netherlands' capital.

And I talked with our travel agent about flights from San Francisco to Amsterdam. She was able to get us a good price on KLM Royal Dutch Airlines. We both liked the idea of traveling on a Dutch airline to Amsterdam.

While Al and I enjoy researching and planning our trips, we use a travel agent for cruise, air and train travel reservations because she's often able to get us better prices than we can find online. She's also aware when cruise lines or air lines offer discounts, and she's able to secure those better prices for us even after we've made our reservations.

Another reason we like to work with our travel agent is that we like having a travel professional available if we run into a problem while on a trip. It's just reassuring to have that extra safety line.

According to Google, it is 5,448 miles from San Francisco to Amsterdam, 584 fewer miles than if we flew directly to Venice. Either way, we're going to be several hours on the plane, and I'm not a fan of flying.

So, next in importance to the cost of the plane ticket is the kind of seat we're assigned. It's vital that Al have an aisle seat, because of his knees and his back. When he's on the aisle, he can easily stand and move around, as he frequently needs to do to relieve joint pain. Also, an aisle seat allows him to adjust his position to relieve the strain on joints. Thankfully, our agent reserved an aisle and middle seat for us. She also arranged to have a wheelchair available for Al, to get him easily from check-in counter to gate.

Since I wanted to save money without sacrificing comfort, I began searching Airbnb offerings in Amsterdam.   The Internet has spawned an entire alternate lodging world in which ordinary people rent out their bedrooms, homes or apartments for prices below traditional hotel rates. While there are several such lodging websites — Vacation Rentals by Owner (or VRBO), HomeAway, and others — I chose Airbnb.

A friend of mine has used VRBO for years and swears by the service. Another friend loves

HomeAway. But my nephew (in his 20s) travels worldwide for business and he always uses Airbnb. He urged me to use the service, too. So I started searching. The search was fun and engrossing.

I went to the Airbnb website (Airbnb.com), typed in Amsterdam, and began perusing the many offerings. I found people who were renting out their couch for as little as $15 a night, while others offered rooms for as little as $47 and as much as $400 a night. Complete apartments ranged from about $165 a night up to several hundred, depending on location and level of luxury.

The prices on Airbnb were far closer to what our budget could absorb than Amsterdam hotels. I emailed several Airbnb hosts asking about their accommodations. I wanted to be close to canals and historic sites, but I also wanted a room that was quiet and didn't require climbing a lot of stairs.

I soon learned that historic buildings in Amsterdam had businesses on the ground floor and residences on the floors above that. So, no matter what, Al's sore knees would have to climb some stairs.

I searched for a room rather than a whole house to save money and also because I wanted to have a host who could help and advise us on seeing the city. I found a wonderful woman with a 17th-century home in the historic Nieuwmarkt area. Mirjam is a graphic artist who has designed books (both the interior pages and the covers) and who designs sets for community theater groups. She sounded like exactly the kind of person we'd love to get to know. Her nightly rate included breakfast.

I phoned our travel agent and asked if she could better the price for a room with breakfast. "In Amsterdam?" she said. "I couldn't come close to that price." So I booked the place. Four nights in Amsterdam at $133 a night.

I began studying maps to see what was near our room. We would not be far from Amsterdam's New Church, nor from its Old Church. Plus the centrally located neighborhood was laced with canals. Excitement rose within me.

Come September, we were going to have four wonderful days in Amsterdam before boarding

Holland America's Nieuw Amsterdam for 12 glorious days on the Med.

At breakfast a few days later, as I was reading the "Dear Abby" column, I heard Al say, "I got an idea last night." I looked up to hear his idea.

"I was thinking that I don't want to arrive in Amsterdam all discombobulated from jet lag and I came up with an idea that might interest you." I waited.

"I think we could adjust our waking and sleeping schedule until we are on European time," he said. "There's a nine-hour difference between California and Amsterdam. We could go to bed an hour earlier and get up an hour earlier each day until we're on European time, and then just stay there. That way, when we get into Amsterdam we'll be on Amsterdam time and there won't be any jet-lag at all. Besides, slowly adjusting our inner clock will be a lot easier on us than flying over and being nine hours out of kilter."

I knew Al wanted to haul along his camera equipment and film (yes, my sweetheart is a film photographer with his own wet darkroom, although he also carries a small digital camera) and he'd want to start shooting as soon as we arrived. I, too, wanted to be fully awake and aware of our surroundings. What fun is it to go somewhere new and be exhausted?

"Sounds interesting. How would we do it?" I asked. Al said he'd cover our bedroom and bathroom windows with tinfoil so no light could get in, and we'd have to wear eye masks.

For a few days we talked about what else we'd have to do to adjust our schedule. For one thing, we'd have to be sure to unplug our phones to keep from being awakened by incoming calls.

It sounded good to me. An interesting experiment. We'd start about two weeks before departure and see if we could adjust our sleeping and waking schedules.

In the meantime, I began searching TripAdvisor and other travel sites to get ideas on what to see in Amsterdam.

Isn't the Internet a marvel? So much information available at our fingertips. In the old days I'd hike off to the library and search through travel guides and other resource books to find out about a place I'd never been. Now I sit at the computer typing in questions, searching out answers, wandering down interesting side-streets, and accumulating file folders full of notes.

By typing the address of where we would be staying into the Google search bar, I pulled up maps to locate our place in relationship to the rest of Amsterdam. I could even pull up a street view and check out the houses along our pedestrian-only lane (Koestraat). It all looked beautiful to me. Cobblestone street, gray stone buildings with bicycles parked near the front doors. And at the end of our lane, a canal.

Whenever Al and I travel to a destination city, we buy tickets to ride the hop-on hop-off bus. We first discovered these tour buses when we were in Washington, D.C., a few years ago. For people with limited mobility or limited energy, these buses are a perfect solution for seeing important sights. The bus route also gives riders a great overview of the city. Along the route are major sights where passengers may want to spend some time. The passengers can hop off and explore the museum or gallery or monument or gardens. And once finished with exploring, simply get back on the bus and ride until they see another place they want to explore.

I was thrilled to learn that Amsterdam has the equivalent with a hop-on hop-off canal bus (boat). So I ordered a two-day ticket for us.

I also signed us up for Van Gogh Museum tickets. I love van Gogh's work and cannot imagine going to Amsterdam without visiting his museum. All the various online tour guides encourage buying tickets ahead of time so that we can skip the long lines (and long waits) for tickets at the museum or gallery itself. Skipping long lines fits our plans perfectly.

As far as other sights go, we would decide once we're in Amsterdam, what else we might want to do.

OUR TIME-ADJUSTMENT EXPERIMENT TO AVOID JET LAG

We begin our time-adjustment experiment 15 days before departure.

Using tinfoil and painter's tape, Al spends part of the morning of Sunday, Sept. 14, covering our bedroom and bathroom windows, to block out all light. As I hear the metallic crinkle of tinfoil coming from the bedroom, I realize that our long-awaited trip is actually beginning here in our comfy Northern California cottage.

If this works, if we're actually able to adjust our inner clocks, we'll arrive in Amsterdam Monday morning, Sept. 29, awake and alert and ready to explore the city.

Our experiment starts tonight, as we climb into bed at 9 p.m., slip on our eye masks and try to sleep. Tomorrow we'll get up at 5 instead of our usual 8 a.m.

Since I can't stand being awakened by an alarm, Al sets up a chirping cricket sound on our iPad to wake us at 5 a.m.

In the morning, when we hear the chirp, we lumber out of bed, trying to act enthusiastic, brush our teeth, get dressed and go to the kitchen for breakfast. I feel really tired, maybe even a little "jet lagged." But we're determined and stumble through our day without complaining.

Monday night we go to bed at 8 p.m., and get up Tuesday at 4 a.m.

Tuesday night we go to bed at 7 p.m. and get up Wednesday at 3 a.m.

Each day, I find myself struggling to stay awake and alert. I don't succeed on the "alert" goal very well. My whole body feels heavy, as if I'm wearing a 70-pound jacket. Whenever I say I feel exhausted, Al says he feels great. So, I simply stagger through the day, hoping to feel more "with it" tomorrow.

By Wednesday night we are so tired that we collapse into bed at 6 p.m. and fall asleep almost immediately.

Thursday, the cricket chirps at 2 a.m.

Thursday afternoon, my brother phones to see how our experiment is going.

"To tell you the truth, I feel a little spacey," I say.

He wants to know what we do during the many dark hours between 2 a.m. when we arise for the day and when everyone else is up and about.

"We turn on the lights and do the same things everyone else does during the day – research on the computer, reading, writing, organizing tasks for later in the day."

His only response is to laugh heartily and wish us well.

Al and I continue adjusting our daily routine an hour a day until we reach Amsterdam time, which means gong to bed at 2 p.m. and getting up for the day at 11 p.m. We will maintain this schedule until our flight out of San Francisco Sunday, Sept. 28.

WEDNESDAY, SEPT. 24, 7:15 A.M.

We've been up for more than eight hours, had breakfast and lunch, and are now getting set to do around-town tasks.

It's actually beginning to feel normal to get up at 11 p.m. By next Monday, when we get to Amsterdam, we'll have been on European time for just about a week. That's when we'll know if this clever experiment has worked.

I will say this: On our first day (when we went to bed at 9 instead of our normal 10 p.m. and got up at 5 instead of our normal 8 a.m.) I felt pretty miserable. But the next night, when we went to bed at 8 p.m. and got up at 4 a.m., I didn't feel quite so out of it.

And each day, as we've moved one hour closer to Amsterdam time, I've been feeling slightly more "normal." However, I have not been able to do much creative work. Just haven't had the energy or motivation. I have mainly done web research, organizational work and stuff like the laundry.

Today Al straps a wristwatch on both wrists. His right hand watch is set to California time. His left-hand watch is set to Amsterdam time. When I ask why he is walking around with two time zones hooked to his body, he responds, "I'm an engineer," as if that answers everything.

THURSDAY, SEPT. 25

Al's 74th birthday is tomorrow, but we're celebrating it today. Tomorrow will be chock full of tasks for the trip, and we want his birthday celebration to be leisurely and pleasant. So at about 8:30 a.m. we head out for St. Helena, a charming little North Bay town where Al wants to enjoy his birthday dinner. Of course, it will really be a birthday brunch (if any of the restaurants or cafes are open when we arrive).

Instead of taking a highway, we drive the back roads. Because of last night's refreshing rainfall, the air is clean and fragrant. The old oaks with their gnarly black branches and mossy green sides look washed and beautiful.

Nowadays, when I ask Al if he's hungry, he checks both his watches. If it's mealtime in one of the zones, he'll say he is. If it's not mealtime here or in Amsterdam, he'll say he's not.

In St. Helena, we consider several restaurants and cafes, and finally settle on one that has outdoor tables.

The Northern California scuttlebutt is that Robert Redford lives in St. Helena (or at least has a home here). So I'm always on the lookout whenever we're in St. Helena. So far, I've seen nothing to confirm that report.

After a delicious birthday dinner (at lunch time), we drive slowly back home. This afternoon, Al revises his packing list for the third time.

SATURDAY, SEPT. 27, 12:25 A.M.

We've been up for an hour and a half and I'm feeling great. Good night's sleep. The bed is completely covered with stuff as we pack and repack. We've both made lists of things we don't want to forget.

I just typed out an emergency call list that includes info and phone numbers incase we lose our credit cards. Al's carrying one and I'm carrying one. We also have phone numbers and email addresses for our travel agent, our next-door neighbor and two family members incase of an emergency. And they all have a copy of our itinerary.

The washing machine chugs away with one last load of laundry before the trip. We've had breakfast. Al made pancakes. There's still a lot of food in the fridge that we have to eat before we leave tomorrow – eggs, yogurt, some left-over chicken, two fresh beets, a little milk in the carton and a little orange juice in the bottle.

We've alerted our credit card companies of our travel plans, and checked to make sure we'll have no trouble using our credit cards on the trip. We've paid ahead on all our monthly bills.

And changed a few hundred dollars into euros.

I can't believe we're so close to leaving. Tomorrow's the big day.

Yesterday Al bought a small flashlight so he won't stumble around in the dark when we're in Amsterdam, should he need to get up in the night. I emailed Mirjam yesterday, giving her our flight number and expected time of arrival.

4:35 A.M.

We're packing. And we're packing. And we're unpacking. I pull out a couple of pairs of slacks and two tops and put them back in the closet. Packing's a little complicated because Amsterdam is expected to be cool and perhaps rainy. However, the cruise is expected to be very warm.

I'm not a fan of lots of luggage. If I can get everything into one wheeled suitcase, I'm happy. On this trip, the goal is one wheeled suitcase and a backpack apiece. The backpack will become our carry-on for the plane.

My backpack holds our most vital information. I have a KLM airlines file with our reservation and seat assignments, a file I've made on Amsterdam with instructions on which train to take from the airport and directions to Mirjam's home. There is information on sights we want to see, our ticket confirmations for the Van Gogh Museum and the hop-on hop-off canal bus, along with our flight reservations from Amsterdam to Venice and a thick file on the cruise and its many ports of call.

Should our bags get lost or misplaced during our flight, we'll still have everything we need to enjoy Amsterdam and get us to the cruise ship.

When the laundry is dry and I start folding it for the trip, I realize anew how much room men's underwear takes up. Their undershirts and shorts are so much thicker than women's panties and bras. Of course, women's shoes can rapidly fill a suitcase. On this trip I refuse to take heels. I've bought a new pair of athletic walking shoes, which I'll wear on the plane, and I'll pack two pairs of sandals – a casual beach-type pair and a dressy pair for eveningwear. They take up almost no room in the suitcase.

The most difficult part of this new time schedule has been mealtimes. We have breakfast shortly after we get up at 11 p.m. (which is 8 a.m. in Amsterdam).

Then I'm hungry at 4 a.m. (which is noon there), but it seems too early to eat lunch. Today I put beets on at 4:30 a.m. and we have a nice lunch with chicken and rice and beets at 5:30 a.m. (which is 1:30 p.m. in Amsterdam)

We eat supper around 11 a.m. It seems so strange, but I know that after our flight tomorrow, it will all make sense.

5 P.M.

Al announces that he's winnowed his packing list to the essentials. "After several dozen revisions, I now have defined exactly what goes where," he says with a look of pride.

Of course, we haven't yet gotten around to packing his clothes – he's just talking about his camera gear, film and electronic equipment. My packing pile includes notebooks, paper and files. His packing pile is all cameras, film and electronics along with baggies stuffed with wires and cords.

We drop into bed at 2:30 p.m. and immediately fall asleep.

Sunday, Sept. 28

OUR JOURNEY BEGINS

Al is kissing me awake. "We overslept by three hours," he says between the kisses. An explosion of adrenalin propels me out of bed and into the bathroom. My inner planner snaps into full gear: I'll quickly have breakfast, then take a bath, then ...

"Well, it's clear we can't count on the iPad to wake us up," he says, his voice thick with irritation, as I frantically plan my departure tasks.

But before I can squeeze toothpaste onto the bristles of my brush, he says sheepishly, "Oh, wait, it's not 5:30 a.m. It's 5:30 p.m." And at that exact moment I, too, notice that we have not overslept. I push open the bathroom window and see that it is still light out. Children's laughter drifts up from the nearby playground. Quickly I head back to bed.

At 8 p.m. I wake up, certain I heard the chirping cricket's call.

"Is it time to get up?" I ask.

"No," Al whispers. "It's only 8. We've got three more hours."

Sleep returns.

The cricket wakes us at 11 p.m. Ahhh, this feels right. Black as pitch outside. And we are ready for the last few hours before departure. Obviously, our excitement kept us from sleeping well. But now, we perform the last of our tasks from taking out the garbage to locking all the windows (and removing all the tinfoil).

After our 4 a.m. lunch, it's one more review of our lists and plans.

At 5 a.m. KLM emails saying our departure has been delayed one hour. Not a welcome message. I immediately email the info to Mirjam in Amsterdam. We will be so tired by 3 p.m. (new boarding time) that I'm hoping we can function. We'll see.

After dropping off our house key at a friend's, we ride the Airport Express Bus to San Francisco airport. I love taking the bus to and from the airport. Love crossing the Golden Gate Bridge in the fog or sunshine, love the ride through Golden Gate

Park and through the Sunset District with its distinctive San Francisco architecture. This morning the ride is smooth and we are eager to get on with the trip we've been anticipating for so long.

At the airport, we check our bags, then look around for a wheelchair. I show the woman behind the counter our reservation, which clearly asks for wheelchair assistance, and she directs us to a waiting area. After 30 minutes, I return to the counter, and again ask for wheelchair assistance, and I am given a slip of paper with a number on it and told to return to the waiting area. This time our wait is only a few minutes.

Then it's off to security and then our gate. While sitting at the gate with our backpacks, Al reads. He has loaded 30 books onto his Kindle for the trip. I plan to take books from the ship's library for my reading. But while we wait for our departure, I walk around, visit the various shops, skim the newspapers and magazines there, wander past the restaurants and in general try to keep myself awake. I'll have plenty of hours to sit on the plane. While I can, I want to keep upright and moving.

We board our 747 at 2:30 p.m. Al and I are among the early boarders, those needing a little extra help to get settled. With almost 600 passengers heading to Amsterdam, the flight attendants want to get us into our seats as quickly as possible. I check our reservation papers and head for our reserved seats in Row 40. But when I reach our seats, a flight attendant says we can't sit there.

"But these are our seats," I say.

"No," she says, and then points us to two inside seats in the center of this wide-body plane. "You're in Row 39, seats E and F," she says.

"Excuse me," I say, showing her our reservation sheet. "Look, we reserved an aisle seat for my husband and the middle seat next to it for me." I point to the numbers on our reservation sheet, but she shakes her head, "No." and insists we squeeze into two tiny middle seats.

She says, "I'm sorry, but they always do that. They just give whatever numbers your agent wants, but those numbers mean nothing. The seat number on your boarding pass is the seat you've been assigned, and your seats are here," she points again to the middle two seats in a row of four.

I glance at our tickets. The seat numbers do not match the numbers on our reservation (made way back in June).

"My husband cannot sit in a middle seat," I say. "He has crippled knees that need the space of an aisle seat."

"I can see he needs an aisle seat, and I'll do my best to help," she says, but I know in my heart there will be no help for us. She continues, "I'll ask if the passenger on the aisle will change places."

"Yeah, like that's going to happen," I think.

She insists we move into the middle seats, and we comply.

We struggle in and squeeze down into the seats, only to find that there is no space under the seats in front of us. Metal posts block what little footroom we might have had. Because I cannot get my backpack under the seat in front of me, I hold it in my lap. My feet go under the seat in front of the person to my right.

By now the aisles are crowded. People try stuffing bags the size of bassinets into overhead bins. Soon the plane is full.

Al and I are exhausted. For us, it is almost midnight and we're ready for sleep, but we're in seats that make comfort impossible. His poor knees are slammed tight against the seat in front of him. I am furious but helpless. Pulling his pain pills from his backpack, he pops one in his mouth, and puts the bottle holding the rest in his pocket.

When the demonstration video begins showing where the emergency exits are, Al says, "No one here could get out of their seat, let alone get out of the plane in an emergency. I'm going to sleep." Then he slips on his eye mask.

The flight attendants ask the passenger on the aisle beside Al, if he'll trade seats, but he won't. Who would? These inside seats are instruments of torture.

My backpack sits on my lap. No flight attendant even suggests I put it under the seat in front of me. The attendants know there's no room under the seat in front of me. And there's no room in the overhead bins.

I am so upset I could explode. I fully under-stand how passengers can go berserk on a flight like this. Yet there's nothing I can do about it. We are in the air on our way to Amsterdam and the seat-torment is our reality for the next 10 hours. I slip on my eye mask and immediately fall to sleep.

During our 10-hour 45-minute flight, we are jostled awake three times, as one or the other of our seat mates gets up. Each time, we take the opportunity to climb out, too. We walk the aisles, use the bathroom, drink some water from small bottles available at the back of the plane, and even-tually return to our torturous seats for more sleep.

AL RECOUNTS OUR KLM EXPERIENCE

When we made reservations for our flight to Amsterdam, I was delighted: we were flying KLM.

Back when the earth was flat and large reptiles roamed free, I worked as a field engineer for a computer company. For my clients in the Netherlands, I flew into Amsterdam, which meant that I flew KLM.

KLM was a wonderful airline. The seats were roomy and comfortable; the food delicious; the customer service impeccable. Every time I flew, I was given a little blue-and-white Delft tile. I had so many I was thinking of re-tiling the bath.

That was a long time ago, but the memories came rushing back when I saw that we were going to be carried to Amsterdam on those beautiful blue wings of KLM.

SFO International was an anthill Sunday morning, Sept. 28. The bus dropped us in front. No curbside check in. We pulled our wheeled bags inside. The line at the KLM counter curled around like a spent serpent. We dragged our bags some more.

Eventually, we reached the counter and checked in. No problem there. When my wheelchair arrived, I was loaded in and we headed for security. Where did all these people come from? It looked like half of San Francisco was being screened. We, fortunately, had TSA Pre "skip the line and stay dressed" passes. Only a quarter of San Francisco was going through that line.

To my delight, the camera bag made it through X-ray just fine. Three cameras, 70 rolls of film, a light meter, kilometers of wire and electrical adapters. And an iPad. No problem.

I, however, flunked. Go figure. Three passes through the metal detector and it still beeped.

"Any metal on you?"

I wanted to say, "I'm a metalsmith—silver in my hair, gold in my teeth, lead in my rear," but I knew that wouldn't fly, so I said nothing. They finally gave up and let me go through.

To our dismay, security and food were on level two; boarding was on level one. There wasn't even a potty in the boarding area. We decided to opt for food.

The closest place to eat was a deli, just above the gate. I had a soggy tuna sandwich (possibly made in China), a brownie and a Pepsi. $15. So much for memories of a pleasant meal before departing.

When we went down to the gate, it was a crowded anthill. When we finally boarded — an hour late — I, in my wheelchair, was let on early. I would need every minute.

Turns out the seat numbers on our reservation didn't match those on our boarding pass. A lively discussion between the cabin attendant and my ever-vigilant spouse ensued. Looking at our reservation sheet, the cabin attendant said, "Oh, those seat numbers don't mean anything. They always get changed."

The seat numbers that KLM had assigned turned out to be two middle seats in a four-seat-wide section. I couldn't do that. Oh yes, I could. It was a full plane and there were no choices. I looked at my seat with horror. How is an adult male supposed to fit in there? There's not enough room. Oh, yes there is. Shut up and eat your kale.

When I finally managed to squeeze in, I discovered that with KLM you don't use the word "seated."

"Inserted" is more appropriate, in the same sense one uses for a suppository.

Now I'm an adult male of modest dimensions: 6 foot 1 inch and about 165 pounds. My seating requirements aren't unusually large. The seat was my width exactly. With my back firmly against the back seat "cushion," my knees pressed solidly against the seat in front of me. There wasn't room for even a newspaper in the magazine pouch. I was pinned in like a bug in a specimen case.

To make things more interesting, there was some sort of metal support under the seat in front of mine, right where my left foot wanted to go. There being no room elsewhere for my feet, I ended up playing footsie with my grumpy seatmate (the one who got the aisle seat to my left) all the way to Amsterdam. Sunny had the same experience on her side.

I pulled out my pain pills and attempted to go to sleep. It was then that I discovered my seat reclined only a tiny amount, perhaps five degrees. That worked to the benefit of the chap pinned in behind me, but it wasn't enough to lean back and sleep. I had no choice: chin-on-chest sleeping for 10 hours. Thank God for pain pills.

And so off to Amsterdam's Schiphol airport, "Schiphol" being a Dutch word that expresses deep gratitude to one's Creator for finally having arrived. And where's the loo?

Looking back at our nonstop flight, all I can say is thank goodness we'd adjusted our internal clocks, so that we were able to sleep on the plane. For the other passengers, it was 2:30 in the afternoon when we boarded. For us, it was nearly midnight and we were exhausted. Thus, deep sleep came easily.

HELLO AMSTERDAM

The 15th century Waag (weigh house) was originally one of the gates in the city wall. It is the oldest non-religious building in Amsterdam.

It's a quick and easy 20-minute train ride from the airport to Amsterdam's Central Station. And we are wide awake. Our experiment worked. Not a wisp of jet lag. The minute our train stops in Amsterdam, we're off for our morning adventure.

Central Station, a huge and beautiful brick building, opened in 1889. It's 19th century Renaissance Revival design dominates the entire area with turrets and ornamental details and stone reliefs.

Trains, buses, trams, taxis and ferries converge comfortably in front of the beautiful station. The main tourist office is based here as well as departure quays for the tourist boats cruising city canals.

Outside, we easily find a taxi. The driver, a man about our age, seems happy to take us to our lodging. As the taxi heads out, my breath is sucked away by the stunning beauty of a huge towered and domed church standing across the sun-dappled harbor. Its large rose window (between two towers) and mammoth Baroque dome are gilded with sunlight. "Look, Al. Look at that beautiful building."

Our taxi driver is amused by my gasp of delight. "St. Nicholas Church," he says. "St. Nicholas is the patron saint of Amsterdam." Then, he adds, "When you come from a young country like yours, I can understand how you can be impressed. But for us, this is just normal."

We all laugh at his words.

Then, as he drives along a canal-side street, through the historic Nieuwmarkt area, he says with a touch of surprise in his voice, "You're staying in the Red Light District."

He stops at the canal end of Koestraat (our street), and lifts our bags from the trunk. "It's just down there," he motions, "on the right side." We slip on our backpacks and start down the street pulling our wheeled suitcases to what will be our home while in Amsterdam.

In less than two minutes, we're standing in front of a black door that bears the address of our Airbnb hostess. We ring Mirjam's doorbell. She hurries down to welcome us. She's a woman about our age with a warm smile and eyes that sparkle through her glasses. I immediately feel at home. She helps haul our bags up her narrow, twisting stairs. Our room is at the back of her house at the end of a private hallway. The bathroom is just steps from our door.

Mirjam gives us a key to the building, a key to her flat, and the Wi-Fi password Al will need for the Internet. She shows us a map of the area, taking care to point out the location of her house, so that we can easily plan forays throughout the historic downtown vicinity. And she answers our many questions. We will see her in the mornings when she serves breakfast in her apartment dining room. Although Al and I are early-morning people, she is not, so we arrange to have breakfast at 9 a.m., which is somewhat early for her and somewhat late for us.

Al is thrilled with our room's good Internet connection. I love the big window above the desk. It opens wide, filling our room with fresh air and sunshine. The house directly across from our room is full of geometric windows – triangles, squares and rectangles. And below our room is a pedestrian (and bicycle) lane. Our spacious room includes a TV, desk, couch and a comfortable queen-size bed.

Al is eager to get outside with his cameras, so we thank Mirjam, pocket the keys and head out for our first day of exploring. It's great to be wide awake in Amsterdam in the morning.

The minute we step outside, the newness of our setting surrounds us. Church bells chime, a slow-steady resonant sound I never hear back in our

Northern California neighborhood. This block-long pedestrian street that will be ours for the next few days is cobbled. Instead of cars, bicycles lean against the walls of centuries-old stone and brick buildings. The cool, fresh air fills our lungs with enthusiasm. We are here and we are wide awake and ready to explore.

We walk to one end of our street and find four swans – three white and one gray – afloat on a mirror-like canal. I compose pictures of the graceful birds, trying different angles with my little digital camera. In the cloud-softened sun-shine and reflected cityscape, the birds appear to float among liquid buildings. Every time a swan moves, the reflected buildings swim in glowing abstract colors.

Al sets up his tripod, takes some light measure-ments, and begins to photograph the scene.

On both sides of the canal, the streets carry bicyclists to their various appointments. Cars and trucks are few, small, and quiet. The resulting hush holds us gently.

While I wander along, sighing at canal-reflections, Al focuses on bridges. Amsterdam has more than 1,200 bridges, large and small, so Sweetheart will have lots of material to work with. When we take the hop-on hop-off boat tour, we'll see many of the large bridges that open to let ships pass.

Here, among the narrower canals, the bridges are made of stone or metal and create lovely reflections in the water. They also serve as parking places for bicycles.

After the bridge photo session, we follow our noses to the nearby fish market, where local fish, exotics and shellfish of every kind are laid out on ice. We can't control our camera shutters as we capture neighborhood shoppers haggling over what surely will become their supper.

Eventually, we realize we're hungry, and head back the way we came in search of lunch.

At the other end of "our street," we emerge into the Nieuwmarkt area where the taxi dropped us off. To our left is a row of restaurants, bars and cafes. We walk along them, soaking in the vibrant midday activity. Across the narrow cobblestone street is a kind of farmer's market, with a "fast food" herring stall at one end, several flower booths, white tents filled with bright produce and booths selling scarves and tourist trinkets.

We choose a streetside table at a little cafe for our lunch spot. Al gets a salmon bagel. I have a ham and cheese toastie (similar to a grilled cheese sandwich).

Directly across the narrow street from our table is a half block of exuberant sunflowers, bright-white carnations, red and yellow roses and, of course, tulips.

Al says, "We began the trip with the airplane flight from hell. But look at where we're having lunch!"

I know exactly what he means. We are in a world so different from our own that we're like children again, full of wonder and the excitement of discovery.

Bicycles whiz by in a muffled cloud of whirring wheels. Everywhere I look, I see people pedaling bicycles. I've heard there are more than 600,000 bicycles in Amsterdam, and I believe it. As we enjoy our lunch, hundreds of the bike riders pass us, going one direction or another. A woman in coffee-brown tights, an espresso-colored mini-dress and a bright yellow business jacket rides past, her outfit almost as brilliant as the flowers just across our street.

The smell of cigars and cigarettes mingles with the fragrance of flowers. Our small lunch table holds a metal ashtray (something I haven't seen in decades back in California). And cigarette butts litter the ground. But there are no loud engine sounds, no angry truck drivers honking their horns or waving their fists. Just people walking or riding their bikes. And folks like us, sitting at a table eating a sandwich.

Every quarter hour, church chimes fill our ears. There is no rush, so we people-watch as golden autumn leaves drop from nearby trees.

I can't get over the architecture. The houses in this historic district are narrow and tall, with big windows filling their facades. And every last house has a most intriguing gable. There are bell gables, point gables, neck gables, spout gables, step gables. Each style has a story and a distinct historic period when it was favored.

Protruding from each gable is a hoisting beam with a hook for pulleys. Because the canal homes are so narrow and their inside stairs so twisty, there is no way for large furniture or, today, items like refrigerators to be moved about inside the building, thus the hoisting beam. Such items are hoisted from street level to upper levels, and pulled in through the window.

We would learn later (on our canal cruise) that houses in the 17th century were taxed on their frontage, so people made sure their facades were narrow. In fact, the narrowest house in all of Europe stands at Oude Hoogstraat 22 in Amsterdam. That tall skinny house is reportedly 6 feet, 7.5 inches wide by 19 feet, 8 inches deep (2.02 meters wide and 6 meters deep).

What fascinates Al (being a former licensed general building contractor) is how these fairy-tale houses lean this way or that. Some lean out over the sidewalk. Some lean back from the sidewalk. Some lean left, some lean right. All the traditional canal houses were built around the 17th century, when Amsterdam was at the height of its world-wide power. They were built on pilings sunk into soft soil. That may explain some of leaning. It is also said that the slight lean over the sidewalk was purposeful to aid in the hoisting of large furniture, so that the furniture would not bang against the house facade and damage it.

Whatever the reason, individual houses lean, and because the houses are built with no space between them, sometimes the weight of one leaning will send others leaning, as well.

The result is a kind of dancing hodgepodge appearance.

From our table, we watch the world pedal by. A young woman in torn jeans and a white lambskin vest pedals past, while at the same time balancing a sandwich and cup of coffee. Men and women ride by with toddlers nestled in baskets fastened to handlebars. An elderly woman in a lavender pantsuit rides past.

There are heavily tattooed men in jeans and T-shirts, and others in business suits and ties. The entire city, it seems, moves by bicycle.

Eventually, we leave our table and wander across to the flower booths. The color and fragrance form a perfect ending for our meal. The delicious, colorful line of booths and tents fills only one small portion of Nieuwmarkt square.

As we wander beyond them, into the large, paved square, we're faced with a monumental old brick building: the Waag (weigh house). Its huge turrets with their cone- shaped roofs make a most dramatic flourish on the half-empty square.

But we're ready for a nap. We'll return to the Waag later.

As we head back to our room, Al ducks into a gelato shop. When he rejoins me on the sidewalk, he has a paper bowl of lime-colored gelato. I take a tiny spoonful and feel the sour-sweet explosion of flavor from my eyebrows to my toenails. I just love gelato and am so surprised to see the real thing here in Amsterdam. I've always thought of gelato as an Italian dessert, but here it is just around the corner from our room.

Back at our room, we stretch out on our bed and drift off to sleep.

AL'S EARLY OBSERVATION ON THE DUTCH LANGUAGE

After a half day of reading street signs and store names, I think the Dutch language has too many vowels. A's in particular. If one is appropriate, two are better. Waag. Straat. Maarlem. Centraal as in Centraal Station. Sometimes you even get a twofer: raadhuisstraat.

It's as though you don't want that vowel sound to escape too quickly. Exhale when you say it, and you're on the way to being a Dutch linguist.

And it's not jut A's: you'll find doubled E's, U's, and the occasional double O. Read ahead, breathe deeply, and let those vowels soar.

All this is good news for Scrabble players. At one time or another, everyone's had one of those Scrabble hands when all you've picked is six vowels and a consonant, yes? Something like AAIIEEJ, for example. In the Netherlands, this would be a winning hand: something to die for. All you'd need is for someone to put down a V or a K that you could tack on to – both letters are very big in the Dutch lexicon – and you'd probably wind up with a seven-letter word and sweep the game.

OUR FIRST EVENING IN AMSTERDAM

After our nap, Al tinkers with the iPad, adjusting its clock to Amsterdam time. I pull out my

Amsterdam folder to see if I planned anything for tonight. I didn't. This afternoon and evening are free for wandering and discovery.

Before we leave our room, I send a quick email to our travel agent, describing our nightmare KLM flight and asking if she can get us a refund.

Then we head out with our cameras and return to Nieuwmarkt and the Waag. This monumental brick and stone building that totally dominates the square was originally one of the gates in the city wall. Built in the 15th century, it is the oldest non-religious building in Amsterdam.

When the city expanded beyond its walls in the 1600s, Nieumarkt square was created, and the gate became a weigh house, where various goods were weighed (and I assume, taxed) before they could be sold in local markets or shops. It is said that the last item to be weighed here, in 1819, was a chest of indigo.

By then, a lively marketplace filled the square, and the old weigh house building with its cluster of medieval towers became a center for various guilds – the blacksmiths' guild, the painters' guild, the masons' guild, the surgeons' guild.

Al and I walk around the Waag, studying its brick walls and craning our necks to view the large second-floor cupola. That cupola was built in 1690 to form an amphitheater where medical students and colleagues could observe dissections and hear lectures.

The Waag is the setting for Rembrandt's 1632 painting "The Anatomy Lesson of Dr. Nicolaes Tulp." Commissioned by the surgeons' guild, the painting and others like it hung for years in the surgeon's chambers on the first floor.

In the 20th century the Waag served mainly as a museum. It also was once a fire station, and for many years stood vacant.

Today, parts of the old structure have been restored, and the first floor holds a cafe and restaurant.

I just love the idea that our room is only a block or so away from the oldest nonreligious building in Amsterdam.

We photograph the Waag from various angles, and eventually wander down side streets to see what we can find.

I can't get over the ever-present cloud of bicycle riders, and the beautiful canals. The dark placid canal waters seem deep and peaceful. Golden autumn leaves float on their surfaces as do swans and mallards. We even saw a grebe swimming near one of the bridges.

The wind ruffles the water and all the reflections prance. As we wander, oohing and ahhing over the canal and street scenes, we find ourselves at the University of Amsterdam. We step through a large gate and enter a covered walkway filled with tables of books for sale. A market of second-hand books.

Being book addicts, we immediately begin browsing and are thrilled to find table after table filled with books in English. Al starts searching through art and photography books.

I ask a man who is arranging one of the tables if this is a special book sale. "No, not at all," he says in perfect English. "We have a book sale going on here every day."

Seeing a coffee-table sized book on the pueblo in Taos, New Mexico, I open it and gaze with love at the photographs. They immediately transport me to Taos, one of my favorite places. I can smell the dust of its summer streets, and feel the chill of winter in its historic plaza.

I remember wandering through the Kit Carson Home and Museum, and the surprise of finding myself at a table next to the famous Navajo artist R.C. Gorman, as we both enjoyed our dinners in one of the local restaurants.

In the old days, I visited Taos every year – for the beauty of the place, nestled as it is in the Sangre de Cristo Mountains, for the artistic history of it, with its many galleries and artist studios, and for the Taos Pueblo.

The Taos Pueblo, just north of town, is a multi-storied adobe housing complex, the only such Native American community in the U.S. to be continuously inhabited for about 1,000 years.

All of this comes back to me as I leaf through the coffee-table book. Here I am on the campus of the University of Amsterdam, breathing the moist air of the Netherlands, and at the same time I am in some way in north central New Mexico, thinking about Kit Carson and R.C. Gorman and the Taos Pueblo.

If I was in Taos, I'd buy this beautiful book. But I do not want to haul any more stuff around on this trip than I've already packed.

Al has several books under his arm.

"Remember that this is just the beginning of our travels," I say, coming up beside him. "And you packed a lot of books on your Kindle."

"I know. I know," he says. "I'm sorely tempted, but I will leave them here."

And he does.

AL'S RETURN TO AMSTERDAM

I first went to Amsterdam in the late 1970s. I was a field engineer, working on a project in Eindhoven, 160 kilometers (about 100 miles) southeast of Amsterdam. Over the course of four or five trips to Eindhoven, I spent many hours in Amsterdam, seeing the sights and falling in love with the city and its canals.

The first time I saw Amsterdam was in the spring. To paraphrase Steinbeck, it was Amsterdam and it was raining.

Herds of bicyclists, unfazed by the downpour, tore past. The spring bloom – tulips mostly – had come to every shop and stall.

Tables all along the Herengracht canal were filled with people also ignoring the rain, sipping coffee and chatting happily in a language I didn't speak, but could yet understand. The air was laden with the perfume of winter's end in a beautiful old city. I was utterly captivated.

During the visits that followed, I grew both more familiar and more in love with the city-by-the-canals. I picked up a bit of the language and explored more of the little alleys and waterways. And then, all too soon, my work finished, it was back to California. Memories of Holland moved far to the back of my mind in the Someday I Will Return file.

Thus it was, when Sunny and I extricated ourselves from our nightmare flight the morning of Sept. 29, 2014 – 35 years since I'd last seen Amsterdam, I wondered if the spell would still be there.

The world had changed, or at least aged, and so had I. It is said that you can't go home again, and Amsterdam had felt like a "home" to me. Hope mixed with apprehension mixed with anticipation as we made our way from airport to Central Station.

When we stepped onto the sidewalk in front of Amsterdam Central, it was all I had hoped and yet other. The imposing bulk of St. Nicholas Church still stood as I remembered it. Herds of bicyclists still roamed *every street. Downtown still opened before me, though filled with new construction. I barely recognized where we were. It was, however, very much Amsterdam. My heart felt relieved.*

Our friendly taxi driver grabbed our luggage and drove us to the end of Koestraat, alongside a canal whose name I couldn't pronounce. Koe, being a bicycle-only alley, required a short walk down to our Airbnb abode. There we were warmly greeted by our hostess and began settling in. It was time to rediscover.

That afternoon, as we walked down the lovely tree-lined canal toward an ancient building called the Waag, the magic began working its way back into my heart. What did the trick were little things. The serene canals, clotted with boats; the tables packed with people talking to one another; the wonderful old buildings, most not quite vertical. A myriad of small canal-spanning bridges connecting uneven cobblestone streets. Microcars parked precariously on canal edges. The herring vendor's cart (spelled "hering"). Yes, Amsterdam had changed and so had I, but I still knew the city, and the city still warmed my heart.

Sometimes you can go home again.

Tuesday, Sept. 30

THE REMBRANDT HOUSE AND THE RED LIGHT DISTRICT

These small, neighborhood canals are almost sensual in their beauty.

T he iPad cricket chirps us awake at 7 a.m. We dress quickly and head outside, determined to see

Amsterdam before the bustling hum of daily business crowds the streets with bicyclists.

Cloud-filtered light softens the view of streets and buildings. There's a kind of hush hovering expectantly over everything that makes us want to whisper rather than talk. Al is eager to show me the Old Church, just a few blocks and one or two canals from our room. And I am eager to see it, the oldest Gothic monument in the city.

I did a little research, and know that the building is huge, about 36,000 square feet. It began as a Catholic church, but from 1566, when the Netherlands turned Protestant, it became a Protestant church.

I know that the church is built over a cemetery and that the floor consists entirely of gravestones. One of those gravestones is for Rembrandt's wife.

I also know that the roof is the largest medieval wooden vault in Europe. Walking to the church is like walking through a series of picture postcards. Everywhere I look is an artist's paradise. White gulls wing silently along canals. Watery reflections add depth and color and wonder to the cityscape. I continue to point my camera and snap.

And then we see it, an enormous stone structure with mammoth windows, standing beside a canal and surrounded by a stone square. Old trees spread their branches, shading the square and providing a sense of comfort and protection.

Both Al and I shoot pictures of the doors, the windows, the beautiful brickwork walls. The church is not open, but signs on the doors show that both religious and cultural events take place here. We learn later that the church has four pipe organs. I can imagine how the windows vibrate when all four are being played at once.

As we make our way around the building framing pictures with our cameras, the sun rises, warming the stone square and the nearby buildings.

AL'S RESPONSE TO SEEING THE OLD CHURCH ONCE AGAIN

The first verse of Martin Luther's 1529 greatest hymn, which some call "The Battle Hymn of the Reformation," aptly describes Amsterdam's Old Church: "A mighty fortress is our God; a bulwark never failing." At the time those words were penned, the Oude Kerk was

already 300 years old. Time has not reduced the impos-
ing majesty of that structure, even if there are newer
and larger churches elsewhere.

This is why, on this day I had to take Sunny across
the Oudekennissteeg *bridge over the* Ouderzijds
Voorburgwal *canal (Dutch names are not for the faint*
of linguistic heart) to see the Old Church. Its stone
walls rise above cobblestone covered streets. It is a
symbol of endurance that's so characterizes the city of
Amsterdam. It is definitely a must-see.

One of the unique aspects of this church is that it
stands squarely in Amsterdam's Red Light District
(the area where prostitution and other sex-oriented
businesses are located).

There is, in fact, a bronze statue not far from
the church's front door, honoring the area's prostitutes. The statue, named "Belle," is full breasted,
standing proudly on her pedestal. The inscription
beneath her reads: "Respect sex workers all over
the world."

When it nears 9 a.m., we head home for breakfast.

Mirjam has a hearty meal waiting for us. Her table is beautifully set with colorful china – yellow plates, bright orange cups, white creamer. We enjoy ham, cheese, croissants and other breads, boiled eggs, jam, fruit, juice and coffee. It not only smells good, it is also nourishing and delicious.

While we eat, she talks about her artistic work and shows us some of the books she has designed. One that fascinates me is for blind children. Its pages are filled with Braille and embossed illustrations. I can imagine little fingers finding the pages fascinating.

Mirjam's late husband had been a fine art photographer. The two of them met when they were both working on a book project: He was the photographer and she was the graphic designer. Several of his pictures hang above the breakfast table, interesting both Al and me.

She also tells us about her son, who is now grown and in the Dutch army. We are staying in what used to be his room. I'm really happy that we chose to reserve her room for our Amsterdam lodging. It is so interesting talking with her.

One of the rewards of travel is the people you get to meet and the stories they tell of their lives. Mirjam's stories enrich my Amsterdam experience.

Shortly after 10 a.m. we head back out into the city. This time we walk to De Nieuwe Kerk (the New Church), located on Dam Square next to the Royal Palace. By now the sun is high and we unzip our jackets as we stride along.

Dam Square, a large 13th-century plaza, was famous in the 1960s as a hippie hangout. Today, restaurants, cafes and shops surround it.

Opposite the Royal Palace stands the National Monument, a tall, white column adorned with sculptures and erected in 1956 to honor victims of World War II. As we approach it, we see TV crews and cameramen and wonder what news event is taking place. But we're eager to explore, so we don't even pause.

As we saunter toward the Royal Palace gazing this way and that at the buildings, a family from Spain asks us to take their picture with the New

Church in the background. They, in turn, take a picture of us.

Madame Tussauds Wax Museum beckons with its statues of historic figures, pop idols and movie stars, but we resist, and instead head for the New Church.

There is so much to see and do, but we guard our energy and Al's arthritic knees, so we carefully choose where we want to spend our time.

By 11:15 a.m. we're ready for a break. We find a little bar named De Spaanse Ruiter and order coffee and biscuits. The air is thick with the smell of rain, but no drops fall. I can see why Al remembered this city with such fondness. Such long-lived beauty, such civility.

After our coffee break, we head back to Central Station, snapping shots all along the way. By the time we reach the bustling transportation center, the sun is out in full strength.

We learn that the huge and stunning Central Station is held up by 8,600 pilings. With about 1,500 trains a day arriving and departing, and with trams and buses and taxis and water buses coming and going, few people have the time to simply stare at the beautiful building.

We hoped to change some of our dollars into euros at the train station, but don't like the exchange rate, so, instead decide to go to lunch. It's always nice to take a food break.

There are so many Amsterdam restaurants – Indonesian, French, Chinese, Spanish – that it could complicate mealtime decisions. We choose a small creperie on Warmoesstraat. Al orders a strawberry crepe. I get a mixed fresh fruit crepe.

The fellow making our lunch says his name is Rami and is from Iraq. He says his family now lives in San Diego. The three of us talk about California while he makes our crepes. Mine is full of banana, strawberries, kiwis.

After lunch, a nap.

And then our afternoon explorations.

THE REMBRANDT HOUSE

Not far from the Waag, we find the Rembrandt House Museum, located on Jodenbreestraat.

Across the road from it, we take pictures of colorful boats in the river. Chimes are playing "Que Sera Sera" over the busy square. The music fills my head with lyrics: Whatever will be, will be. The future's not ours to see.

A small, loud motorboat adds its putt-putt to the chimes, and two grebes chase each other chirping noisily.

We take our pictures from the midst of a bicycle parking lot. There must be hundreds of bikes parked here – black, pink, blue, red, yellow, green. Bicycles are so prevalent in Amsterdam, that there's even a three-story bike parking garage next to Central Station. It's actually a tourist attraction, and a magnet for photographers.

This city has bicycle lanes, bicycle traffic lights, bicycle rental places and plenty of bicycle parking lots.

Eventually, we extricate ourselves from the bicycle parking lot, cross the street and check out Rembrandt's handsome three-story house. This is where the great artist lived and worked between 1639 and 1658.

As you no doubt know, Rembrandt is considered one of the greatest painters and printmakers in European art, and the most important in Dutch history. His realistic portraits, his use of light and shading for dramatic effect, his penetrating, introspective style make his work exceptional.

I remember him from college art classes, but know little about him apart from his name. Our afternoon tour of his house enlarges my awareness.

Although there are no paintings of his on display here, the house itself and its furnishings are as they were when he lived and worked here. The building itself teaches so much about him and his work.

Our tour begins with a video of his life. So much sadness! His first three children died in infancy. His wife, whom he dearly loved, died at 29 after giving birth to his son Titus, his only child to reach adulthood.

Later, he had a mistress who sued him and to whom he had to pay alimony.

Titus died a year before he did.

A later mistress bore him a daughter, and that daughter named her son after Rembrandt, thus ensuring the continuation of the painter's name.

After the video, we receive a hand-held audio guide. We punch in the number of the room we are in and get a lively description of what went on in it when Rembrandt lived there.

We see his kitchen, his living room, his studio, his etching and printing workshop and a room filled with objects he collected – statues, weapons, fabrics, shells and all sorts of other things.

My favorite room is his studio, a large, well-lit space where he made his paints and where he painted his pictures. It is complete with chalks, charcoal, easels and brushes.

The studio docent explains in detail how Rembrandt developed various shades of red with linseed oil and pigments and how he used the various shades to create depth in his paintings.

We learn that Rembrandt worked with only 14 different hues.

The Rembrandt House also includes his etching and printing workshop, where docents explain and demonstrate how he made his etchings. We can make an etching in the same way he did, but Al is running out of energy, so we skip it.

The museum houses an exhibition of almost all 250 Rembrandt's etchings along with paintings by his contemporaries.

I'm fascinated with the fact that there are no bedrooms in the house.

It seems that in the 17th century, people had "box beds" that resemble elaborate cabinets or armoires. Rembrandt's was in his living room. The cook's was in the kitchen.

The box beds were very short because people thought if they laid flat the blood might rush to their head and kill them. So they reclined on numerous pillows in their cabinet-like box beds. Can you imagine!

We spend about two hours in the museum and love every minute of it. Although there is no elevator and the stairs are narrow, it's a wonderful afternoon outing. Well worth the 12.5 euro entrance fee.

AMSTERDAM'S RED LIGHT DISTRICT

As we wander the area around our place, it's obvious we're in a sexy neighborhood. We understand that the Red Light District – about an acre and a half of narrow lanes, shops, cafes, bars, restaurants, brothels, sex shops and prostitute windows – comes to life late at night. But we're exploring the streets only during daylight hours, and the entire area seems very low-key.

I'll admit the signs advertising massage parlors or sex clubs are artistically graphic, and many a shop window displays "toys" we can neither identify nor imagine how to use. But the streets are quiet as we ramble through.

Prostitution is legal in Amsterdam, a city priding itself on its liberal and tolerant attitude. Although the Red Light District is filled with peep shows, clubs, bars, even a sex museum, during the hours we're sight-seeing, it's pretty sleepy.

Al and I chuckle over shop window displays of engorged plastic penises, vagina-shaped suckers and all sorts of candy underwear for him and her.

There are Red Light District tours: late at night the atmosphere here can be quite electric.

Window prostitution is unique to Amsterdam. Unlike a brothel, where customers go inside to view the goods, window prostitutes appeal directly to their potential customers.

Buildings along many streets and lanes have large street-side windows through which self-employed prostitutes display themselves. The room behind the floor to ceiling window is hidden from view by thick scarlet drapes. However, when the prostitute who rents the space is ready for clients, she'll open the drapes and display herself in the window. She might sit in a chair or on a bar stool. She might stand beside a pole or coat rack. She might tap on the window to get the attention of some passer-by.

After dark, the Red Light District is bathed in red neon lights.

Today, in the soft light of early morning, all the scarlet curtains are drawn closed across the windows.

On one window a hand-written note announces: "Sex workers do not want their pictures taken. Please refrain from photographing these windows."

Some window prostitutes hire what might be called bouncers to patrol the streets and make sure no one takes pictures of the windows and the women in them.

As the afternoons lengthen and evening approaches, the draperies open and the women behind the glass prepare for work. Yesterday evening, when we were heading home, I glanced in a window and saw a beautiful young woman. She could have been 28 or 30. She was tall, with thick, blond curls hanging slightly below her shoulders.

She was completely clothed, but I could easily see her full curves.

She was arranging furniture in the window and gazed out just as I gazed in. Our eyes met. I gave her what I hoped was a friendly smile and nod, and her lovely face opened. Her lips returned a restrained smile, her eyebrows rose in a friendly way and I'm sure her eyes twinkled.

This all happened in a moment. My impression was, what a lovely woman. That was my first impression of Amsterdam window prostitutes.

Today I have a completely different response. We pass a window displaying a nearly naked woman who is so thin she looks as thought she might be starving. Above her pierced navel I can easily see her ribs. I wouldn't be surprised to see her backbone rippling through her stomach.

She wears the briefest of brief black bikinis. Her chopped black hair makes me think of a head full of explanation points. A tattoo circles her upper arm and shoulder.

She stands swishing her boney hips side to side and then thrusting them forward and back – exuding a darkness and chill that feels a little frightening.

I have no idea how business is for the two window women. But I wish them well and hope they can maintain their health and their dignity in a "profession" that is both old and dangerous.

Farther along the way, we come upon a scooter store. One of the scooters has a bumper sticker proclaiming: Home fucking is destroying prostitution.

That gives us a good chuckle.

AL RECALLS THE RED LIGHT DISTRICT OF YESTERYEAR

It was on one of my early engineering trips to Amsterdam that I first found the Red Light District. Decades ago. Things were a bit ... shall we say "looser" back then.

In those days of yesteryear, the ladies of the district were strong proponents of "Loont het om te adverteren," which is to say "It pays to advertise."

And how, you might ask, does – did – a woman of the evening advertise her talents, then and now?

For the answer, one need only consider the nearest automobile dealership. There, the expensive, beautiful new models are displayed on the showroom floor. There are, of course, more-basic models on the lot, but they're not in the showroom. The dealer would rather you bought top of the line.

And so it is in Amsterdam. The lovely ladies of the evening may be seen in windows along the streets of the district, somewhat modestly attired, coyly inviting you in.

In days of yore, there was much more lady and much less modesty. Think of displaying a new car with the hood open so you could see the engine's large carburetors. You get the idea: We'll leave it at that.

It is, today, considered nekulturny, to use my favorite Russian word – someone so identified is considered to be well below "uncultured" – to stare. But one is free to imagine. Call it a mental test drive, to get back to the auto analogy.

But the district isn't just windows and ladies. No. There are also stores. Stores filled with plastic toys. Toys for every gender, number of participants, occasion, or activity. This was all new to me. In days of yore, there were women and there were ... clubs ... and all was as it had been since the Hittites.

Today, one can safely say that technology (and better, plastics) have greatly enlarged (no pun intended) the opportunities for entertainment. For the strolling tourist, there is much to see. Just be prepared for the inevitable question, "Mom, what is that thing?" Time to feed the swans, son.

Wednesday, Oct. 1

THE VAN GOGH MUSEUM

The path to the Van Gogh Museum leads past these murals. The museum houses the largest collection in the world of Vincent van Gogh's works.

Up at 7 a.m. and out to photograph and bask in the beautiful city before breakfast. Then breakfast and a friendly conversation with Mirjam. She tells us how much she loves being an Airbnb hostess. It provides her with extra income and she has a whole new circle of friends made up of other Airbnb hosts in the city. Today, in fact, they are all holding a birthday party for one of the hosts.

Today and tomorrow Al and I will see Amsterdam from the city's canals. They have been part of the landscape since the early 14th century, but the canal ring we'll traverse was constructed in the 17th century.

I love the idea of spending two days sailing along a Unesco World Heritage site. The historic Canal Ring (three semicircular canals that form a ring around the historic city hub) received the World Heritage designation in 2010. And this is where we'll spend today and tomorrow.

There are many canal cruise companies in Amsterdam. Our two-day pass is with Amsterdam Canal Bus and offers three routes: green, red and yellow. Each takes a slow and gentle journey through a specific area of Amsterdam and provides a running commentary in Dutch and English, describing the history and meaning of what the boat is sailing past.

Amsterdam Canal Bus has 16 stops including the Anne Frank house, the Maritime Museum, the zoo, the Rijksmuseum, the Van Gogh Museum, Vondelpark, Dam Square, the Rembrandt House, Nemo and some others.

In addition to daytime canal cruises, there are evening cocktail cruises, dinner cruises, an afternoon/evening pizza cruise and a Dutch candlelight cruise that includes artisan cheeses and wines.

We board the green line at Central Station. It's a good thing I bought our 34-euro tickets online ahead of time, for there are many people waiting to buy theirs. By the time they get their tickets, the boat is full and pulling away from the dock. They'll have to wait about a half hour for the next boat.

Our boat is low and long, like a floating limousine. The padded seats are comfortable. Some are open to the air, others protected by a window covering. All the open seats are taken by the time we board. The seating arrangement reminds me of a railroad train dining car – two bench-style seats with a table in between. The tables work well for Al and others carrying large cameras or large bags.

Out into the old harbor we go, where we get a good look at Central Station and the three-level bicycle parking garage from the water. Then our boat enters the Prinsengracht (Prince's Canal) through the Unicorn Lock. Unicorn is one of 16 locks built around the city in the 17th century to control the water level in the canals and protect Amsterdam against the sea.

The Prinsengracht is the outermost canal of the historic ring. Named after the Prince of Orange, it's a tranquil waterway through a historically wealthy area of town. As we skim along and crane our necks to see important buildings, I think what a privilege it is to spend today and tomorrow in a living museum. For that is what Amsterdam is.

Lots of passengers get off at the Anne Frank House stop.

Al and I have one goal today, and that is to visit the Van Gogh Museum. As we sail along, headed for the museum (which contains 200 paintings, 5,000 drawings and 700 letters from the tragic and brilliant artist), we pass the Western Church, the Northern Church, the Houseboat Museum and many other sights.

As we glide along, we learn that the canals are nine feet deep, that there are 63 miles of canals and more than 1,250 bridges. Every time we float under a bridge with a 16th century date on it, Al comments. This place is changing his (and my) idea of "old."

We float past scores of houseboats lining both sides of the canal. More than 2,500 houseboats claim Amsterdam's canals as home. Some houseboats look like they were designed by architects. Others appear to be homemade boxes plopped on the cluttered decks of barges. They all look romantic to me.

The most interesting houseboat I learned about was De Pozenboot (The Cat Boat). It got its start in 1966 with an abandoned mother cat and her kittens.

Today hundreds of cats live on De Pozenboot, which has been designed specifically for them. Volunteers feed and care for the felines, whose waterborne home meets all the legal requirements for a modern animal sanctuary. In 1987 it was registered as a charity: the Cat Boat Foundation.

There's something very soothing about floating slowly under old stone bridges. Even though we're in the heart of a huge metropolitan area, here on the canal, it is quiet and peaceful. No wonder the people in the 17th century wanted their homes to face the canal.

I'm not sure how long it took us to reach our stop at the Rijksmuseum and the Van Gogh Museum, but I think it was about half an hour. The Rijksmuseum (the national museum dedicated to the arts and history of Amsterdam) is an imposing structure and looks as though it could be the cousin of the Central Station. It is huge. We know that it holds the world's largest collection of Dutch Masters paintings, including works by Rembrandt, Vermeer and others, but our focus today is on van Gogh.

We cross the highway, walk through a large covered walkway where a cellist is playing hauntingly beautiful music and emerge onto parklike grounds behind the Rijksmuseum.

Here, a large sculpture spells out "I Amsterdam." The "I" and "Am" (of Amsterdam) are red. The rest of the sculpture is white. People throng the sculpture, clamoring on top of the letters to stand and mug for their friends, or squeezing through the letters or leaning casually against them as they snap selfies. Everyone is having fun with the tall, long-lettered sculpture.

I get Al to stand between two of the letters while I take his photo. Later we learn that there are several such sculptures scattered around Amsterdam as tourist promotional pieces.

The Van Gogh Museum is quite a walk back through the park and then right to Paulus Potterstraat 7.

Once again, I'm happy to have our "skip the line" tickets in hand. The ticket window line is more than a block long. We're able to go to the "already have my ticket" door and get right in.

I have loved van Gogh's paintings ever since I was a kid and saw his "Irises" and "Sunflowers" and "Starry Night." Loved his wild skies and vibrant landscapes. To me his dynamic work is so intense it's almost alive. My favorite van Gogh painting is "Café Terrace at Night" and it is here, so I'll be able to stand and absorb it to my heart's delight.

The museum has three floors of van Gogh's paintings, and an elevator. I'm able to get Al a wheelchair. With a wheelchair, we can spend as much time as we want enjoying the place without Al's knees and back giving out.

Among van Gogh's famous works that we get to enjoy are "The Potato Eater" (1885), "The Yellow House in Arles" (1888), "The Bedroom" (1888), several self-portraits and still lifes, and one of his last paintings, "Wheatfield With Crows" (1890).

We love seeing the various phases he went through as he developed his unique style. Love looking at his different experiments. Love learning how he was influenced by the Impressionists. His Asian-style paintings fascinate us.

And, I always find the correspondence between him and his brother, Theo, so moving. How blessed he was to have a brother who believed in his artistic genius and who supported his work.

Besides his famous paintings of sunflowers and irises and wheat fields, I see one I'd never seen before: "Almond Blossom," painted in 1890 to celebrate the birth of Theo's first (and only) child. It is a delicate work of almond tree branches bursting with blossoms, against a bright blue sky. It's intensely joyous.

By the time we've seen everything we can, we're hungry. We find the cafe and discover more than snacks. You can get a snack or a sandwich. Or you can enjoy a full, delicious meal prepared by chefs wearing tall, white hats.

We each order fish, rice and grilled fresh vegetables. And a slice of apple pie for dessert. A most satisfying meal. And what makes it even better is that every table in the cafe holds a vase bursting with sunflowers. We spend at least an hour savoring our food and the setting.

We are both rather surprised to learn that Vincent van Gogh painted for only about 10 years. In that brief span, he made about 900 paintings. And sold only one. His younger brother Theo, who was an art dealer, saw the brilliance in his work and supported him both financially and emotionally. Theo died just months after Vincent, and the two are buried side by side in Auvers-sur-Oise, France.

Those of us who love van Gogh's work have a woman to thank for preserving and promoting it.

His sister-in-law (the wife, then widow, of Theo) made it her life's mission to promote his paintings and drawings and to organize, translate and publish the extensive correspondence between the brothers. Were it not for Johanna van Gogh-Bonger, we most likely would never have heard of the artist Vincent van Gogh.

Widowed after a short, happy marriage to Theo, Johanna was left, at 29, with a year-old son, and Vincent van Gogh's entire life's work – more than 2,000 paintings, sketches and drawings, and about 900 hand-written letters between the brothers.

Although some of van Gogh's contemporaries admired his unique and powerful paintings, the common consensus was that they were rubbish, the work of a lunatic, and Johanna might just as well burn them.

She, however, felt they were brilliant and deserved to be recognized as such.

Theo and Johanna had named their son after his artist uncle: Vincent Willem. He was 1 when Theo died.

Johanna moved herself, her son and all of Vincent's artworks and letters from Paris back to the Netherlands, where she spent 34 years promoting his work and correspondence.

Because of her lifelong effort, Al and I and everyone else can enjoy the intense beauty of this powerful painter.

During her lifetime, Johanna arranged more than 100 exhibitions of his work. And her son, Vincent's namesake, took up the torch, establishing the Vincent van Gogh Foundation, and being instrumental in establishing the Van Gogh Museum.

And here we are, sated with Vincent's paintings, our minds and hearts basking in the beauty he created, in the museum his namesake nephew helped establish. Life feels good indeed.

After lunch, we wander the museum gift shop, admiring the books, the elegant silk scarves bearing van Gogh paintings, the ceramics and artwork, but we leave it all there and head back to the boat stop, where we'll catch our next canal bus.

We ride the green line boat, although we could take the red line from here. There's a cool edge to the afternoon air, and we're glad to get a window-covered seat as we sail through shop-filled neighborhoods. Along our afternoon canal cruise I spot a Museum of Bags and Purses. Wouldn't that be fun to explore!

For the remainder of the day, we cruise canals through old and beautiful neighborhoods, sailing under stone bridges, gawking at shops and shoppers, and end up cold and hungry. We leave the boat at the Rembrandt House Museum stop. We both remember a corner restaurant we saw yesterday close to the museum.

Yesterday, we thought it looked inviting. Today, with the evening air chilling us, we're eager to see what Rembrandt Corner's menu offers.

Inside, the place is warm, and we happily shed our jackets. The polished wood, the glowing lamps and large windows all create a feeling of welcoming coziness. I'm ready for something warm and comforting. And then I spot it on the menu: traditional Dutch pea soup. When the waitress comes to our table, I ask about the pea soup.

"It's wonderful!" two women sitting at a nearby window chime in unison.

I see they each have a bowl.

"You've sold me," I say to them. Al and I order the soup.

Then I ask the women, "Where are you from?"

"San Francisco," they chime together.

The four of us get into a wonderful conversation about San Francisco and Amsterdam. The women are nurses in town for a conference. They have only today free and are so glad they get to see a few sights, but wish they had more time because Amsterdam is such a fascinating place.

"You'll just have to come back," I say, and they agree.

When our supper arrives, the aroma cups us like loving arms. One spoonful is all I need to know I've entered pea soup heaven. The thick, flavorful green is chock full of chunky potatoes and carrots. Its warm deliciousness fills me and makes me happy.

Thursday, Oct. 2

THE DE GOOYER WINDMILL

De Gooyer Windmill, the tallest wooden mill in the Netherlands, is one of only six such windmills still standing within the city limits.

W e sleep like rocks. Our iPad cricket wakes us at 7 and we're soon dressed and out on the street.

The fragrance of baking bread fills the morning air.

As church bells chime, we head past the Waag and enter a street we've never been on before. It's jam-packed with restaurants. Bright signs compete for my eyes' attention: Sushi Café, Eat Mole, Little Saigon, Chinese, Argentinian Steak House, a deli, Dim Sum, Thai, Brood Bakery, Restaurant de Portugees, several Indonesian restaurants, a Malaysian restaurant and a Japanese place advertising noodles.

We wander aimlessly, watch shopkeepers wash their windows and open their stores. We watch as small panel trucks unload supplies, or take on trays of fresh-backed bread.

At breakfast, I tell Mirjam about the street crammed with restaurants serving all kinds of foreign foods. She says there's a common saying: "You can eat in all languages in Amsterdam." How true it is.

After breakfast, it's off on our second day of exploring Amsterdam by canal bus. Today we'll take the red line. I especially want to see the De Gooyer Windmill and according to the map that came with our tickets, the windmill stop is only on the red line.

We know the drill, and are among the first to board our boat, grabbing an open-air seat. Our seatmates (a young couple on the other side of our table) say they're from Heidelberg, Germany.

"We had six hours driving from home," the husband says. They are thrilled to be fulfilling one of their dreams – to see Amsterdam from its famous canals.

The wife adds, "We're both very interested in art. That's why we've come to Amsterdam."

Al and I share with them what we can about the Van Gogh and the Rembrandt House Museums.

Our boat sails out into the old harbor and past the Bimhuis concert hall. We've heard wonderful things about the jazz and improv musicians who play here. If we had more time, we'd attend a concert.

Our boat enters the Herengracht (Gentlemen's Canal), which connects the harbor and the Amstel River. The Amstel is the city's only natural waterway. It's the river that Amsterdam is named after.

We pass the famous science center Nemo, the Maritime Museum and the Artis Zoo and are heading toward the De Gooyer windmill, when our boat takes a turn and goes in another direction.

At the next stop, I walk to the front and ask the captain what's going on. He says the windmill is no longer on the route because of some construction that is taking place. Our best bet is to get on the green line, ride it back toward Central Station and get off at Nemo. From there we can walk (about a half mile) to the windmill.

So that's our new plan.

We sit back and enjoy the ride, listening to the commentary as we float past canal houses and under stone bridges. Eventually we find ourselves at the Rijksmuseum and Van Gogh Museum stop, and climb off. In a few minutes, a green line boat arrives, and we climb on.

By the time we get to the Nemo stop, it's almost mid-day and we're both hungry.

Nemo is a green, five-story building that looks like the hull of a great ship. It is the largest science center in the Netherlands and is filled with hands-on science exhibits.

Approaching it, we can hear the squeals of delight from hundreds of children inside. It reminds me of the Exploratorium in San Francisco.

You could easily spend a whole, fun day at Nemo. But I want to see the windmill, so we'll simply have lunch here and then head for De Gooyer. It turns out to be quite a hike. Luckily there are benches along the way, and we're able to sit and rest as we go along.

There used to be windmills throughout Amsterdam, but now there are only five or six left. The De Gooyer is the most central of those that remain.

Once a corn mill, today it is a brewery where folks can enjoy a wide selection of hand-crafted beers.

When we finally reach it, we find the windmill is an octagonal wooden structure on a stone footing. Its dark brown walls look weathered yet strong. And it is big – about three stories high, with sails that make it look even taller.

Built around 1725, it was the first corn mill in the Netherlands to use streamlined sails. We take several pictures and then head back to the

Maritime Museum stop, where we'll catch the red line and ride to Central Station, then walk home.

Even though we haven't spent much time at the windmill, it's rewarding to see the historic structure and to know that the brewery attracts many tourists and locals. I don't think our visit to Amsterdam would have been complete without seeing this muscular old windmill.

We're back home by 4:30 p.m. This is the social hour, the time of day after work when all the sidewalk cafes fill up with people ready for a drink and some conversation. Dinner comes much later. But we can't wait for the normal dinner time – somewhere around 8 p.m.

We have supper at an Indonesian restaurant Mirjam recommends and enjoy marinated grilled pork with ginger, stir-fried broccoli, pepper, carrot, corn and mushrooms, and rice.

After dinner, we meander in the growing darkness, soaking in the lovely atmosphere of beautiful Amsterdam.

During our brief visit here, we've shared Italian, Chinese, Dutch and Indonesian cuisine, plus lots of crepes and gelato. We've relished the vibrant street life, the interesting Red Light District, the canals, churches and museums.

Speaking of museums, once we're back in our room and we've packed for tomorrow's departure, I glance through some tourist information we picked up along the way and see that there are many museums in this city that I would have appreciated visiting if we'd had the time. Here's a partial list from the tourist brochures:

Houseboat Museum, Photography Museum, Purse and Bag Museum, Torture Museum, Erotica Museum, Marihuana Museum and Amsterdam Museum. We'll just have to come back.

Friday, Oct. 3

VENICE, HERE WE COME

Al finds our stateroom comfortable.

Up at 5:35 a.m. Mirjam has coffee for us. Then she helps haul our bags downstairs, and the three of us walk to the end of our lane where our taxi is waiting – a white car, trunk open, parking lights flashing in the silent darkness.

Mirjam made sure the taxi was there – one more detail she so graciously arranged. A quick hug, and we're in the car heading for Schiphol Airport.

Our young driver is talkative. He says his day starts at 5 a.m. He's from Turkey but has lived in Amsterdam for 16 years. He loves the city because it has a lively nightlife and "everything is easy here."

At the airport, Al says our driver pushed 85 miles per hour all the way. Because the freeway was empty, it didn't seem that we were going that fast.

Because of fog, our flight is delayed two hours. This concerns me. I'd planned that we'd be in Venice by 11 a.m. That would give us enough time for a Grand Canal cruise and a quick look at St. Mark's Square. Now, I doubt we'll have time for that. But I still hope.

By 10:30 a.m. we're airborne. Again, our flight is with KLM. However, this 737 is far smaller than the jet we flew on out of San Francisco. This one holds about 130 passengers (instead of nearly 600), and it is not full. Al has an aisle seat and I have a window seat and we're happy as clams.

The clouds below look like thick whipped cream. We'll be in Venice in an hour and a half. I can barely wait. All my memories of that city are glittery, shimmering, bright and beautiful.

Halfway through the flight, we're served coffee and a waffle cookie snack. Just perfect.

The clouds clear as we near Venice, and we can see the city in its entirety, all red tile roofs, floating in the Adriatic. Built on an archipelago of 117 small islands, Venice was at one time the most prosperous city in Europe. Today it is simply the most beautiful.

At the airport, we follow Holland America guides to the bus that will take us to our ship. Unfortunately, it takes forever to get everyone on the bus. So we sit and wait. No Grand Canal trip today. Sigh.

When we finally arrive at the ship and are checked in and receive our room key card, it's well after 2:30 p.m. In addition to missing the Grand Canal and St. Mark's Square, we also missed the onboard meet-and-greet gathering where we might have made connections with other passengers.

Because of the fog at Schiphole, and the ripple-effects of that delay, our plans have changed.

We're so hungry we head immediately to the lido for lunch. A bowl of fresh spaghetti. Then a smaller bowl of ice cream. Al also has a cream puff. He's in dessert heaven.

OUR CABIN

After lunch, we find our cabin.

On past cruises, we've chosen the least expensive cruise ship lodging, inside rooms. But for this cruise, we reserved a veranda stateroom. Inside rooms are smaller and have no windows. Our veranda stateroom is larger and comes with a balcony.

We booked this more expensive room because of the balcony. Sailing past Venice and Greece, and along the Bosphorus Strait in Istanbul will offer many sights we may never see again, and a private balcony view is just what we want. We can imagine the pleasure of sitting on our balcony in our pajamas enjoying a cup of coffee, and watching the beautiful world pass by.

To give you an idea of cruise ship lodging: On this cruise an interior room is about 150 square feet and costs about $1,000 per person. An interior room has no windows.

Our veranda stateroom is about 220 square feet, includes a sitting area, floor to ceiling windows, and a private balcony. We've paid $2,559 each for it.

There are other cabin choices including ocean view, which is more expensive than an inside room but less than a veranda stateroom. And there are a number of suites available, each with additional space and additional amenities.

A cautionary note: The cruise prices shown online or in brochures, usually do not include port fees and taxes. If you're trying to develop an accurate budget for your trip, be sure to ask what those additional fees are. As a rule, the more ports your cruise ship stops at, the more fees and taxes you will pay.

We're eager to check out our room: Cabin 7029, on the starboard side (right hand side) of the ship

When we step inside, we're more than pleased. The colors exude luxury. The floor-to-ceiling windows fill the place with light.

We stretch out on our queen-size bed and find it comfortable. The room also has a couch with a table just perfect for room service meals, a desk and seat, flat-screen TV with DVD player, and a wall of windows that allow us a generous view of passing scenery. The door in this window-wall opens to our balcony. The balcony holds two chairs with cushions, a coffee table and a tiny, round table perfectly proportioned for two coffee cups or two wine glasses.

Drinks, both alcoholic and nonalcoholic, fill our small refrigerator. There is a charge for any drinks consumed, and the fridge will be kept fully stocked throughout the cruise.

Each of the bed's side tables has two small drawers and a shelf. There is sufficient closet space for our hanging clothes. And one of the closets (the one with the safe) has cubbies for folded clothing.

This room comes with an important bonus for me – a bathtub.

Back in the old days when I worked in an office, I appreciated the efficiency of a morning shower. But since retiring, nothing beats a bath. I love luxuriating in hot, sudsy bathwater. And for the first time on any cruise we've taken, I'll have this privilege.

Two white robes hang beside the bathroom. We'll use these during the cruise, and can take them home as souvenirs for a price.

A first for us is the power cutoff at our cabin door. Beside the door is a cabin key card wall slot. Our cabin steward shows us how it works. When we enter the cabin, we slip our room key card (the size of a credit card) into the wall slot and that turns on the power. When we leave, we take the card out of the slot, which turns off all the power.

A lovely arrangement of fresh yellow daisies and a bottle of champagne adorn the top of our desk. The small card accompanying the flowers and champagne says they are compliments of HAL. How sweet is that? We suspect this pleasant greeting is ours because of our travel memoir, **Cruising Panama's Canal**, *Savoring 5,000 Nautical Miles and 500,000 Decadent Calories.*

That cruise was also aboard a Holland America vessel. And the book has received praise from readers and travel bloggers. We mailed a copy to Holland America's president, so we suspect the flowers and champagne are a "thank you" gesture. And we're happy to have them in our room.

Since we don't drink alcohol, I phone the front desk to ask if the champagne can be exchanged for sparkling apple juice and am assured the switch will be made.

Before long, we hear the lifeboat drill announcement and make our way to the lifeboat deck. I'm always reassured by these pre-cruise drills. Through them, we learn exactly where to go if there's an emergency, how to put on our life-preserver jacket and what to expect from the lifeboats.

Every passenger is required to go through the drill. If you try to dodge it, you'll be escorted from the ship.

At 4 p.m. sharp, our ship, the Nieuw Amsterdam, heads out along the Giudecca Canal. It's a gentle departure in full afternoon sunshine, passing waterfront hotels and long lines of stone apartment buildings painted in pastel shades of yellow, orange, beige and gray. In the background, church spires and bell towers lean slightly above a sea of red tile roofs.

We pass Santa Maria della Salute, a Baroque basilica built during the plague, either to beseech Mother Mary for her help or to thank her for her help during the scourge.

Then we float past the most famous square in Venice – St. Mark's Square – with its 325-foot tall bell tower, with the Byzantine domes of St. Mark's Basilica, and the long, lacy-Gothic exterior of the Doge's Palace.

Stretched out in front of the palace is a line of black gondolas riding the choppy waters, waiting for tourists to climb aboard.

We sail past a wooded, gardenlike area (so rare in this city where every inch of land has been created from mudflats and swampy islands) and out into the Adriatic.

Once at sea, with water all around, Al and I begin to acquaint ourselves with the ship that will be our home for the next 12 days. Exploring the ship helps ease my disappointment about arriving late and missing a cruise down the Grand Canal. We'll do that when we come back.

So off we go to see what's on each deck.

On the Main Deck (Deck 1) we find the Showroom at Sea. This 890-seat theater includes two levels of balconies, and wonderful art – photos, sculptures, collages. Red is the dominant color. A ceiling full of tiny lights adds twinkling excitement.

The atrium, front desk, shore excursions desk and future cruises desk are all located midship on Deck 1. Although I reserved four shore excursions through our travel agent, Al and I often get answers to our ports of call questions at either the front desk or the shore excursions desk.

Our favorite deck – the Observation Deck – is Deck 11. Why do we love Deck 11? Because the library is here. And the library is our favorite public place on a cruise ship.

Between Decks 1 and 11 are decks with restaurants, lounges, shops, the casino, meeting rooms, the movie theater, swimming pools, the spa, the fitness center filled with treadmills, rowing machines and other equipment, and many decks filled with staterooms.

The ship is truly a floating resort.

We linger in the library. One wall contains an espresso bar called the Explorations Café where (for a price) we can get espresso drinks.

The library itself contains about 1,000 books organized under topics such as best-sellers, travel, leisure, fiction, classics, biographies. Subcategories include political, religious and large type.

There are comfortable couches and chairs throughout the library, along with tables for two and larger tables where people assemble jigsaw puzzles.

Twenty-one Internet workstations cluster between the library and the espresso bar. Here, cruisers can check their email, keep in touch with social media friends and do other Internet tasks.

We don't use the Internet while onboard because it is so expensive: 55 cents to 75 cents a minute, and you must buy a package of minutes. Also, we've found that onboard Internet is so maddeningly slow that we burn up our precious pennies just waiting for messages to appear on screen. But I see plenty of people using the computers, so it just depends on how important being connected is to you.

I find a table for two near the windows while Al orders two lattes and two chocolate croissants at the espresso counter. We are charged for the lattes, but the croissants are included in our cruise.

Not far from the library is the Crow's Nest, an over-the-bow area where people can sit and watch the ship make its way. In the evening, the Crow's Nest is a nightclub with live music and dancing. During the day, it's a gathering place for folks who love to read and watch where the ship is going.

In the afternoon, team trivia and other games are played in the Crow's Nest. It's a great place to meet and mingle in a fun and casual atmosphere.

We sip our lattes and enjoy our croissants while gazing out the window at the beautiful sea. I never tire of watching the ocean and its constantly changing hues.

After checking out the ship and getting our bearings, I have to say that the Nieuw Amsterdam feels sleek and sophisticated. Its art collection — paintings and sculptures and multimedia works as well as antique clocks — enliven walkways and public spaces, and the ship itself has clean lines, an Art Deco feel with a modern edge.

Eventually, we return to our cabin to spend most of the afternoon on our balcony, with the fresh smell of ocean filling our nostrils. Al reads his Kindle. I write in my notebook and think about how wonderful it will be when we visit the Acropolis.

I was there only once before, back in 1980, when my mother and I took a tour of Athens and surrounding areas. On one of our unscheduled days we went to the Acropolis.

She had dreamed of seeing Greece ever since she was in grade school. Back in those days, the kids studied Greek mythology in elementary school, and her heart had been captured by the stories of gods and goddesses. When I discovered an affordable Greece tour, she quickly signed on with me.

Our afternoon at the Acropolis turned out to be one of the most memorable events of that trip. However, the stairs to the top were a nightmare — uneven, slippery, steep. I recall Mom having to stop several times on our way up and back, to rest and catch her breath.

Because of that stairway memory, when I scheduled Al's and my tour of the Acropolis,

I made sure there is an elevator for folks with limited mobility. I'm so pleased that Al will actually be able to ride to the top. There's no way he could make it up the stairs I remember.

And if there's one thing you don't want to miss in Greece, it's the Acropolis.

This afternoon slides by with clear blue skies, warm temperatures and pale turquoise water. Relaxation dominates all else. And as the sun turns the horizon golden, we head for the dining room. We request a table for two and take our time with the meal.

Neither of us is hungry enough to order an appetizer, although there are some tempting ones on the menu.

I enjoy vegetable curry with rice. Al has chicken breast with couscous. We both like our dishes. For dessert I have crème brulee and Al has Viennese apple strudel.

As we've aged, our appetites have diminished. The portions served in the dining room are perfectly suited for us. For those with more robust appetites, the dining room meals are not limited to one serving only. I've seen many men ask for two entrees. And Al has often had more than one dessert.

You never have to leave hungry.

Back in our stateroom we discover a chilled bottle of sparkling apple juice, a plate of chocolate-covered strawberries and a reservation for a complimentary dinner at the specialty Italian restaurant (Canalletto) for later in the week.

As Al opens the juice, I call the front desk to find out who gave us this lovely first-night-on-board present. Turns out it's from our travel agent. Obviously, she got our email about the KLM flight from hell. Knowing her, this is her way of trying to compensate us for our misery. Thank you, Maureen!

We take our drinks and strawberries out to the balcony. After toasting love, we settle into a warm and peaceful silence while the moon casts its light across the sea.

What a marvelous beginning to our cruise.

Saturday, Oct. 4

AT SEA

One of many richly satisfying desserts we enjoy on this cruise.

We start our day with breakfast in our room. Room service is included in the cost of our cruise. Veggie omelet, toast and coffee for me. Orange juice, dry cereal, blueberry muffin and coffee for Al.

We receive everything we ordered, plus extra milk.

About a liter of milk, to be precise, labeled in English, French and German: Milk. Lait. Milch. We stash the additional milk in our room refrigerator. It will come in handy when Al brings home some of his extra desserts.

The breakfast spread is attractively served on china, with cloth napkins and beautiful silverware. Our breads come in a nice basket, and the whole thing arrives with a vase of real flowers — pink and lovely

We enjoy our meal with the curtains wide open and the beautiful ocean dancing just outside.

After breakfast, it's off to the library. I do a little more exploring and find a whole section filled with games and jigsaw puzzles. Chinese checkers and chess are all set up on a nearby counter, ready to be played.

People are perusing the bookshelves. Others occupy couches or chairs, reading or working on their laptops. Several are using the ship's computer workstations.

Folks line up at the espresso counter for cappuccinos and lattes and pastries. The steamy sound of the espresso machine keeps up a staccato background beat.

Since our first stop on this cruise is Katakolon, Greece, I pull a Greece travel book off a nearby shelf to learn a little about the place. I see that this seaside village is close to where the ancient Olympics began. Just about the time Al brings a latte for him and a hot chocolate for me, we hear the captain announce over the intercom that tomorrow's stop at Katakolon has been scratched because of bad weather. Instead, we'll go straight to Athens, and have more time there.

I know some passengers will be disappointed with this change, but I'm thrilled. I love Athens, and want to share as much as possible of this wondrous city. Athens, the birthplace of democracy, the hometown of Socrates. Athens, with its elegant ruins and glorious Parthenon hovering high above the city. By canceling Katakolon, we'll get a day and a half in Athens instead of just a day. Yippee!

As I gaze around the library, my heart fills with happiness. I love all the books and the people checking out the books. Couples and individuals sampling books, showing one another something they've just read. Folks recommending this book or that one.

Perhaps my exuberance springs from the sweet and rich hot chocolate I'm savoring.

But I've always loved the way total strangers are drawn into conversation by their love of books and authors.

I watch an older bearded man in a forest green sweater jacket and brown trousers looking up something in a large tome's index. He uses a hand-held magnifying glass. Al used a magnifying glass for several weeks until I mentioned that he could buy reading glasses at the corner drugstore. Now he has a stylish pair that helps him decipher the ever-shrinking type in newspapers, magazines and books.

At 11 a.m. we head for the theater, to hear the ship's shore excursions manager and the location guide talk about the various ports of call we'll be stopping at on this cruise.

When we arrive, the place is packed. Evidently, everyone onboard also wants to hear this presentation. Turns out, it's a one-hour commercial for HAL's shore excursions.

A huge screen displays slides of each place where we'll stop during this 2,666-mile cruise. The descriptions of the various shore excursions make me want to take them all.

Quite a few people leave before the presentation ends. I suspect they're a little peeved at the way the speakers urge us to buy shore excursions. Despite the hard sell, Sweetheart and I stay 'till the end because we're learning a lot about each stop.

At noon we head to the lido for lunch. Thai chicken soup, Peking Duck, rice and roasted veggies. Al, of course, has dessert. Two, in fact: a frosted square of chocolate cake and a lemon bar.

AL'S FAVORITE TOPIC – DESSERTS
When Elizabeth Browning wrote, "How do I love thee? Let me count the ways," she could have been speaking

of my heart connection with dessert. It is impossible for me to precisely date the origin of my infatuation with the best part of a meal (indeed, who needs the meal when you have dessert?)

The initiating event, though, may have been my Grandmother's apple pie (not to dis her loganberry version, for sure).

Gramma's pie began with a from-scratch crust made with Crisco. It was so light it would have floated away were it not held down with a huge pile of sliced green apples I'd picked that very morning. She'd load in the sugar and cinnamon, top it with a lattice crust, and bake it in her trusty old wood-fired Wedgewood stove. When it emerged at the pinnacle of browned perfection, you could hear the cherubim singing. Loudly.

On such a firm foundation was my love for Things Sweet built. Over the years, I've savored a pathway through the astounding variety of dulces human culture has crafted. It seems clear that my affection for confection is well shared across the planet.

Even my broccoli-adoring spouse has been known to eat a piece of my (dare I say?) excellent chocolate cake with triple fudge frosting.

For such as I, to cruise is to pass through the very gates of dessert Heaven. Like other vessels we've sailed, the Nieuw Amsterdam provides boundless opportunity to indulge one's sweet tooth – and variety to match. We're on a cruise! What's a few (thousand) extra calories? Our dentist is back on the quay, and the ship's clothing store has XXL sizes. It's time to go for the gusto – and the Sacher torte while we're at it.

In 2012 when Al and I took our Panama Canal cruise, we were pleasantly surprised to find a daily digest of The New York Times. The eight-page, 8.5-by- 11-inch digest included news, sports, business and an opinion piece. Just perfect for a breakfast read.

I wonder if this cruise provides such a publication. We go to the library to find out, and are told that there are several newspaper digests distributed daily: The New York Times, The Australian Times and papers in Spanish and German as well. They're available at the front desk, just outside the lido and in the library. But the library has already run out of them today.

Al decides to stay in the library and read while I go down to the front desk and see if I can find any copies there.

There's a long line at the front desk, all kinds of people with all kinds of questions. I see no newspapers, but get in line to ask just in case there are some squirreled away somewhere.

While standing there, a lively conversation starts behind me about visiting Athens. It looks like a group of friends all worried about possible dangers in this foreign and unfamiliar place.

I glance at them. They appear to be about my age, mostly women, so I feel comfortable offering some memories from when my mom and I were there. "Just grab a taxi and go down to the Plaka," I say, "and look around."

But they've all heard horror stories about pickpockets, and the stories have grown in their imaginations, and now they're worried that if they don't pay for an organized tour, they may become victims of crime.

"Go in a group," I suggest, "and stick together."

There's a tall man among the many worried women. His eyes twinkle beneath his baseball cap and he says he and his wife plan to check out the Plaka on our added afternoon in port.

"Have you been there?" he asks.

"Decades ago," I say. "Came with my mom. And we went all over the place. We even took a local bus up to Delphi for a day. Just went to the bus station and got tickets. And neither of us speaks Greek. We just figured it out."

He nods, clearly interested in what I'm saying.

Several of the women in his group look doubtful.

"You're a brave girl," one of them says.

I laugh. "You're going to love Athens," I say and then walk up to the counter to ask about The New York Times.

I'm told although the paper is usually out before 10 a.m., the copies disappear quickly. Al and I will have to make sure we get to the front desk or the lido early enough to get a copy.

Back from my foray, and there's a new bottle of Champagne and a plate of chocolate-covered strawberries waiting in our room. Another surprise!

Again I call the front desk to ask if we can switch the Champagne for sparkling apple juice and am told the change will be made. When I ask who sent us this lovely surprise, I'm told the guest relations office.

"Please convey our appreciation and delight," I say. I'm assured that our thanks will be conveyed.

Whatever the reason for these unexpected gifts, I'm happy to accept and enjoy them.

In the afternoon, we go back to the Showroom at Sea Theater for a lecture on Greece and Turkey by the ship's location guide, Tom.

He talks about Athens being the cradle of democracy. He talks about the Acropolis. He says that Athens is named after the goddess Athena, and I remember the myth that she was born from the head of her father, Zeus.

Tom talks about the Plaka, the oldest part of the city, spread out below the Acropolis. He says that there are hundreds of small shops there and restaurants and that it's a perfect place for shopping and people watching.

He talks about Istanbul, the only city to straddle both Asia and Europe, our second port of call.

We will sail from Greece through the Aegean Sea to the Dardanelles Strait. This 42-mile-long strait will lead us to the Sea of Marmara. We'll cruise for six hours through this sea that separates the European Turkey from the Asian Turkey, to the Bosphorous Strait and Istanbul.

The 19-mile-long Bosphorous Strait connects the Sea of Marmara with the Black Sea.

Tom describes Istanbul's museums, mosques and palaces. He says the Grand Bazaar is beyond description, and urges us to visit at least one carpet making shop to observe the ancient art of carpet weaving by hand.

And he emphasizes that everyone, especially women, must dress conservatively while in Istanbul. That means no tank tops and no shorts. People should at all times cover their shoulders and knees. And if we enter a mosque, we women must also cover our heads.

✡✡

Tonight is a formal night, meaning dressy attire in the main dining room. Those who prefer to dress more casually eat in the lido or order room service.

Formal nights give passengers the chance to have professional portraits taken. Studios are set up in the photo gallery area of the ship, offering passengers a variety of backgrounds for their portraits. These formal portraits are not included in the price of the cruise, but as a personal souvenir, they can be priceless.

After dinner (and portraits) everyone heads for the theater and the first big production show of the cruise.

Upon entering the theater, passengers are greeted with glasses of champagne. Al asks for something nonalcoholic and our drinks are quickly replaced with elegant glasses of ginger ale. We find good seats and I watch the beautiful people come in.

Women in gowns and sparkling jewelry. Men in tuxedos. They pause at the top of the stairs, searching for the right seat, and then descend to the row they've chosen. It's like a red-carpet stairway. Couple by couple, the theater fills with cruisers in all their finery.

One couple looks especially like royalty. They're both tall and trim. He has a handsome head of thick, well-groomed white hair.

Her dark hair is stylishly short. She's wearing an off-the-shoulder, nearly backless silk top of gold and creamy brown. It drapes beautifully, flowing like liquid as they walk. They choose seats near the orchestra, then turn and watch for friends. When they see who they're watching for, they wave, and another formally attired couple descends the stairs.

We're in a big, beautiful theater filled with men in crisp black jackets and women in silky blouses and glittery gowns. There are, of course, many passengers dressed less formally, but the entire celebratory scene makes me feel happy.

Tonight's program will be a big song-and-dance production celebrating the City of New York.

Our ship – the Nieuw Amsterdam (which, of course, was the name of New York before it was changed to New York) – has all sorts of artwork giving a tip of the hat to America's largest city. There's a floor-to-ceiling apple sculpture across from a set of elevators. There are photos of Jackie

O strolling the streets of New York, and in the lido there's an entire wall of Andy Warhol's artwork.

So we are primed for an evening of songs about New York.

Before the show, however, the captain and his top brass introduce themselves. They stride on stage to form a long line of sharp uniforms and bright faces.

Captain Bas van Dreumel stands in the middle. And the ship's crew stretches out on either side, everyone from the staff captain, the culinary operations manager, guest relations manager, dining room manager, executive chef, event manager, hotel director, chief engineer, cruise director and purser to the executive housekeeper, beverage manager and shore excursion manager.

As the captain describes their duties, a waiter bearing a tray of drinks walks by, handing each officer a glass. When introductions have ended, the captain welcomes us passengers aboard and, raising his glass in a toast, wishes us all "a safe and wonderful cruise."

After all of us in the theatre have lifted our glasses and taken a sip, the captain says, "I want to point out that I am drinking water, so you can consider me your designated driver."

We laugh and cheer, and then finish our drinks as the officers walk off stage. We're able to stash our empty glasses in holders built into the arms of our seats.

And then the evening's celebration of New York begins. A song and dance presentation designed to show how talented the ship's performers are, this show explodes with high-energy enthusiasm.

At one point in the program, which is really quite good, Al leans over and whispers: "All this dancing and singing is exhausting me."

For me, what's missing is Frank Sinatra's famous song: "New York, New York." I was sure they'd open with that song, and when they didn't, I suspected they'd close with it. But no. It never shows up at all.

Following the closing number, Sweetheart and I wander back to our room. After a hot bath, I don my comfy robe. Al's already wearing his, and we pull out the iPad for a game of Scrabble.

As we play we can feel a windy storm outside and hear the ship groan slightly as it sways.

Sunday, Oct. 5

ARRIVING IN GREECE

A Plaka rug shop displays its wares.

After a great night's sleep (I like sleeping when the wind blows), I pull open our balcony curtains and sunshine pours in. The bright blue sky sprinkled with tight little clouds forms a "good morning" backdrop as we dress and head for breakfast.

In the dining room we're led to a table for four at which another couple is already seated.

As we take our seats, I recognize the man from yesterday's conversation at the front desk. Although he's not wearing a baseball cap this morning, his eyes still sparkle.

His name is Percell. He and his wife, Tina, are from Phoenix. In the old days, she had been a food editor and writer for Redbook and McCalls magazines. I tell her we have a connection because "in the old days" I'd received some very encouraging rejection letters from Redbook. She laughs.

During breakfast, we share our stories. Percell had started out pursuing medicine in college but ended up in sales. Now he owns a packaging company that serves clients worldwide. I can tell he's a great salesman. He's personable. He listens. He laughs. He shares insights and intriguing stories.

Tina grew up in Manhattan. She was an enthusiastic ballerina during elementary and middle school. He grew up in Virginia. They lived in

Seattle for 23 years. I share that I lived in Seattle for four years back in the 1960s.

I love finding common links.

We talk about last night's show, each of us playing theater critic. We describe what we liked and what we could have done without. Al makes a wisecrack about the amount of energy expended on stage. And when I say that I can't believe they did a whole show on New York without singing the song "New York, New York," Percell laughs heartily.

"That's exactly what I thought," he says.

Breakfast with them is so pleasant, sharing personal stories, talking about books and movies and lingering over a third cup of coffee, that we decide to go to the Plaka together this afternoon. We'll meet at 2:30 and grab ourselves a taxi.

Back in our room, Al and I enjoy our balcony as we study the ship's daily newsletter, Today on Location. It describes in detail today's events and activities. We get the newsletter every night when our cabin steward prepares our bed and leaves fresh towels for the morning. We glance at it before going to sleep, but really study it in the morning after breakfast.

Now, I see, that at 11 a.m. in the Culinary Arts Center on Deck 2, there will be a demonstration of how to make hummus and pita chips. And, of course, everyone there will get some of the fresh-made hummus and fresh-baked pita chips.

We woke up too late for church service today (both Mass and interdenominational services were available on board this morning). But among today's many activities – from workouts at the fitness center to a card players' meetup in the Half Moon Room or a class for PC owners in the Digital Workshop – I see there's a half-hour lecture in the Ocean Bar: 30,000 years of art history in 30 minutes: From cavemen to Picasso. It starts in just minutes but will be over in time for me to make the hummus demonstration.

These sound like my kind of events. "I'll meet you back here at noon," I say heading out the door. "Unless you want to meet at the hummus and pita chips demonstration."

Al shakes his head, no. He's reading on the balcony and says he'll be there when I return.

I love the 30-minute art lecture. Although I know some of what is being presented (especially when the speaker talks about Rembrandt and van Gogh), I learn a great deal. And the talk is filled with humor, always a welcome ingredient.

The lecture is also a way of enticing passengers to attend the onboard art auctions. Al and I will not be going to any art auctions because we have no space for more art at our house, and we don't want to spend our money on shipboard art (although we have in the past, and we've been happy with our purchases). Art auctions, while fun and interesting, can add hundreds or thousands of dollars to the cost of a cruise.

I love the hummus and pita demonstration. My opinion on the samples can be summed up in one word: Yum!

At lunchtime, we again go to the dining room rather than the lido. I should probably point out that the lido, where you serve yourself in a buffet arrangement, is not the place to become acquainted with other cruisers.

The tables are smaller than in the dining rooms and most people simply eat and run. In the Manhattan Dining Room we're seated and served by waiters, making the meal a restful, drawn-out affair. However, the food is great in both places.

At lunch we're seated with a couple – Hazel and Bob – from Quebec Province. She's a retired nurse. He's retired from the Mounted Police. They've traveled all over the world. They say they love cruising.

We share opinions about cruising, Holland America and other cruise lines we've been on. The conversation and the good food make for a pleasant lunch.

Afterward I swing by the shore excursions desk to double check on tomorrow's Acropolis tour. I want to make sure there's a working elevator for Al.

The woman behind the counter says, "There is a lift, but it's pretty rickety. And it doesn't always work."

"Let's just hope it's working tomorrow," I say. "Because if it isn't, we can't get to the top."

The expression on her face is both concerned and doubtful. But she says to let our tour guide know that we're the couple needing the elevator. I assure her I will.

At 2:30 p.m. we join Tina and Percell. We all leave the ship and walk along the pier to where a number of taxis are waiting. Whenever we get off the ship, we check out with our room key. When we return, we check in with our room key. That's how the ship knows we're back on board.

Percell and Al clarify the cost of the trip into town, and then we all climb in and head for the Plaka.

The Plaka, Athens' oldest neighborhood, is a labyrinth of narrow streets and alleys and Classical architecture. A perfect place to wander with a camera.

Clustered against the northern and eastern slopes of the Acropolis, the Plaka is also known as the "Neighborhood of the Gods." Most of the Plaka's streets are closed to automobiles. Our taxi drops us at the lower end of a street named Lysikratous.

As the four of us head up the street's gentle slope, we pass crumbling buildings covered in graffiti and ivy. But their decrepitude looks artistic to our eager eyes, and we snap photos as we go.

People pack the Plaka – couples, singles, families. They're sitting at outside cafe tables or they're perusing the shops. The shops are crammed with stuff: painted icons, clothing, jewelry, hats and bags, masks of every size, hand-painted ceramics, post cards and refrigerator magnets and so much more.

It's all fascinating because it's different from what I see back home. That's one of the things I love about traveling — seeing new places and new things (even when they're centuries old). I love gazing at the stone ruins or looking at all the hats and vases and sculptures and various trinkets in the stores.

A little girl plays a concertina, adding lively music to the mix of sounds. Al used to play the accordion, filling our home with toe-tapping tunes. As we pass her, he drops some coins in her case, a small token of appreciation from one musician to another.

Restaurants and cafes squeeze in among the shops, their tables taking up stretches of the sidewalk and the street. Every chair is occupied.

We pause, gazing back down the street we just climbed, and see the Arch of Hadrian and other ruins at its foot. When we wander back, we'll explore these beautiful stone reminders of the Roman days of Greece.

As we pause to look around, the sky darkens and raindrops start to scatter the crowds. The four of us duck into a restaurant and grab a corner table, with windows overlooking the tourist-jammed streets just outside.

Since we all ate lunch on the ship, we're not really hungry, but we're happy to be off our feet and out of the weather for a few minutes. Al gets a Greek coffee. I get iced tea. Percell orders a designer coffee and Tina gets hot tea. We talk and laugh and watch the weather.

Percell and Tina live in Arizona. Al and I live in California, and here we are, enjoying tea in Athens. It feels like magic to be here, half a world away from home, visiting with new friends, in an ancient city filled with ruins from an even older age.

Before we finish our drinks, the sky clears and the light rain stops.

When we emerge, the air is clean and sweet beneath a fresh blue sky. Fat cats – black, white and orange – pick their way confidently through the tourists, their little paws artfully dodging the shallow puddles.

We wander narrow alleys, check out hats in one store, shirts in another. As we slowly wander down toward Hadrian's Arch, we come upon a young boy playing a stringed instrument. The boy looks no older than 10 and his instrument resembles a guitar, but it isn't a guitar. I wonder what it is. I think the tune he's playing is the theme from "Zorba the Greek."

As we approach, he begins to sing in the most lovely plaintiff voice, so beautiful and so earnest I cannot help but drop a few coins in his instrument case. As they fall, he says in perfect English, "Thank you."

When my mother and I were here so many years ago, we took a tour to Corinth, Rhodes, Knossos and the canal that connects the Ionian and Aegean seas. The Nieuw Amsterdam offers similar shore excursions, but I love just wandering on our own seeing what we can see, taking pictures and just being kids again in a place that's brand new to us.

When we reach the bottom of Lysikratous, we wait for the crossing light and then walk across the crowded and busy Amalias Avenue, to Hadrian's dramatic arch.

This all-marble, 60-foot high arch, erected around 131 BC, stands right beside the highway. Buses and trucks and taxis and cars rush by just feet from it. Beyond the arch a grassy, parklike area holds the ruins of what once was the largest temple in the city: the Temple of Olympian Zeus.

Of the temple's original 104 Corinthian columns, only 15 remain standing in a cluster that could take your breath away.

And when we turn and gaze back up to the top of Lysikratous Street, we see at the other end where we ducked out of the rain, the Acropolis. The Parthenon peeks over the cliff's edge, keeping an eye on us all.

✪✪

After a quick dinner in the lido, Al and I head to the theater, arriving early enough to get a good seat for the 8 p.m. show.

Tonight Lance Ringnald, a gymnast who participated in the 1988 Olympics, performs. His acrobatic act uses aerial silk – long ribbons hanging from the ceiling. He climbs these bright red ribbons, wraps them around himself and performs a number of acrobatic exercises 12- to 15-feet above the stage, all the while giving us a running commentary on what he's doing. The act is not only visually stimulating, but his descriptions are fascinating and his stories are funny.

I think how appropriate it is to have an Olympic gymnast performing while our ship is anchored at Greece, where the Olympics originated.

VISITING THE ACROPOLIS

We see the Parthenon and other Acropolis monuments before the crowds arrive.

Breakfast in the bustling lido. Long lines at the customized omelet station and the croissant and sticky bun station. I love the Muesli served here. I add sliced bananas and a cup of coffee and have a perfect breakfast.

Al's got our shore excursion tickets for this morning's visit to the Acropolis, along with two cameras and a collapsible tripod. I have my little digital camera and my note pad. Last night we heard that nearly 1,000 passengers are going on various shore excursions today. No wonder the lido is packed.

Our shore excursion (Athens & the Acropolis) cost $79.95 apiece. This guided tour will get us to the Acropolis early, before the crowds, and will also take us by bus to the Olympic Stadium. Our shore excursion description says we'll see city sites such as the Royal Palace, Constitution Square and will drive past the Temple of Zeus (where we were yesterday afternoon).There are tours that cover more and cost more, but this half-day tour is a good fit for our level of energy and our pocketbook. It is scheduled to leave at 8:30 a.m.

We're at the theater (from where all shore excursion folks leave) by 8:15 a.m. The place is full. A man at the front with a microphone directs each tour group to its waiting bus.

Within minutes, our group is summoned, and we file out, leave the ship, walk along the pier to our bus, and climb aboard. I am excited about seeing the Acropolis again and sharing it with Al.

Shortly after the bus pulls out, our tour guide begins telling us about Athens. It is the capital of Greece. It is named after the goddess Athena. The owl of Athena had blue eyes. Ancient Greek coins had an image of the owl on one side and Athena on the other.

She says that Athens is an open-air museum. "You can see the ancient past everywhere," she says. And her description of the city is perfect. It's definitely a bustling metropolis, but everywhere you look, you see the "bones" of its ancient past. And they are stunning!

When we reach the appropriate parking lot, we get off and follow our guide along the base of the Acropolis. It's quite a hike. She talks about Yani and Maria Callas and Onassis. All of these familiar Greeks called Athens home at one time or another.

She shows us where she wants us all to meet by noon. She says it will take us 20 to 30 minutes to climb the Acropolis stairs. I hurry to her side and say, "We're the couple who needs an elevator."

She nods, and leads us to a uniformed man close by and says, "He will take you to the lift. We'll see you at the top."

Al and I follow the man around a corner and up a rise of steps. Glancing ahead I see something I don't quite understand. Ahead of us is the 260-foot cliff, honey-colored in the morning sun, rising straight up into the sky. And fastened to it is a kind of metal track. What could that be? I wonder. Certainly not the Acropolis lift. It looks nothing like an elevator. Yet, the shore excursion woman's word "rickety" comes back to me.

The uniformed man introduces us to a woman standing next to this metal track. She pushes a button, and a tiny, open-sided box rattles down the track toward us. It doesn't look large enough to hold more than one person.

AL AND THE ACROPOLIS LIFT

My beloved was excited to learn that the Acropolis, the most important ancient site in the Western world, has an elevator for those of us with limited mobility.

Researching it on the web back home in California, she had found this statement: "Due to the nature of the elevator, visitors with cardiac-related disabilities or vertigo-related situations may be denied use of the elevator."

And she'd told me about the shore excursion desk person saying that the elevator was rickety and not always operational.

But the important news was that there is an elevator. My response: Sign me up! I've already had cardiovascular events (several, in fact) and I'm not vertiginous, so what's to fear?

This morning, as Sunny and I followed a uniformed fellow around the base of the Acropolis toward where we would find the lift, I stopped to pant. Looking ahead, I saw it: the elevator.

When you were a kid, did you own an Erector set? Or your brother, or one of your friends? One of those kits with lots of metal bits and bolts and nuts. You could build a Ferris Wheel or a crane or something like that. If you know what I'm talking about, you know what I just glimpsed – the Acropolis Lift.

Tacked irregularly to the cliff side like a barely clinging steel vine, the elevator's track stretched straight up 260 feet.

Fastened to that track and slowly descending toward us (as we watched in open-mouth astonishment) was the lift's cage. And a cage it was, resembling something built for a bird. A bird with minimal regard for personal safety.

When it stopped at ground level, the elevator operator, a petite Greek woman, opened the wire-mesh door and motioned us in. It was a tight squeeze: The word intimate comes to mind. When she stepped in and closed the "door," it was even more intimate.

The morning breeze blew through, and Sunny squeezed tightly against me, eyes slammed shut. I expected to see an icon or a religious statue, perhaps St. Christopher, but no such luck.

The operator pressed the up button, and our little cage was off. Slowly.

As it climbed the cliff, a variety of strange mechanical noises began: squeaks and creaks, scrapings and rattlings. The cage shook and shuddered. Sunny pressed more firmly into me, her eyes tightly shut.

I looked out and saw a marvelous view of Athens and the sea beyond. Our ride to the top was better than anything Disneyland can offer: the ultimate E-ticket ride, for sure.

In the 1970s, there was a small Canadian airline called Pacific Western: PWA. It was said (with cause) that PWA stood for "Pray While Aloft." I'd say that phrase was great advice for us as we inched up the cliff. And pray I did. To my great joy, our prayers were heard, and with one heart-stopping lurch the lift stopped at the top. Gracias a Dios, or however you say it in Greek.

Eat your heart out, you sweaty, stair-climbing tourists: We're here before you! Now let me out!

Several hours and hundreds of photos later, it was time to go down to the bus. We took the stairs.

As we step from the lift, and look around, the Acropolis appears golden in the morning sun. Thank goodness we are here early. There are very few others here. Al and I are awestruck.

As the UNESCO World Heritage Center has said, the Acropolis and its monuments are universal symbols of the Classical spirit and civilization. They form the greatest architectural and artistic complex in the Western World.

This seven-acre limestone plateau is home to four major monuments: The Parthenon, Erechtheion, Propylaea and Temple of Athena Nike. All built in the glory days of the fifth century B.C.

The lift drops us off (maybe not the best use of words) closest to the Erechtheion and its Porch of the Caryatids (Porch of the Maidens). We are instantly captivated by the five beautiful maidens supporting the southwest corner porch's roof. Carved from marble, their gowns drape gracefully as the morning sun sets the whole scene alight. How do sculptors make stone look like silk? I'm awestruck.

Originally there were six maidens, but one was removed by the British in the 19th century.

This elegant marble building is the newest temple on the Acropolis and as we gaze at it, we hear a nearby guide tell a fascinating legend about what happened here.

It seems that both Athena and Poseidon wanted to be the exclusive deity of the city. Their competition was so extreme that they almost began a war. But, instead, the king and the city's citizens held a contest where both Athena and Poseidon could display their powers by offering a gift to the city. The people (and, presumably the king) would decide which gift was the best. And the winner of the contest would be rewarded the city itself as the grand prize.

Poseidon (god of the sea) took his three-pronged sword and powerfully struck the ground. Out of the earth bubbled a fountain. The people were impressed and rushed forward to drink from the water. But it was salty.

Athena then quietly knelt and buried something in the earth. An olive tree sprang from that spot – a much more useful gift. She won the contest, and the city became Athens in her honor.

To this day, near the Porch of the Maidens, grows an olive tree — Athena's gift. It is said that Greece has more than 100 million of these trees.

We are so busy photographing and exclaiming over the beauty of the place that we lose track of our group. It doesn't matter. All we want to do is take pictures and sigh over what we see.

The morning sun is warm. White clouds scatter themselves across the blue sky and all of Athens spreads out below us.

We gaze over the edge of the Acropolis, look-ing at the miles and miles of buildings below.

I remember coming here with Mom so many years ago. We were able to get much closer to the Parthenon's columns than is allowed today. I remember Mom talking to a guard about his work and about the wonder of the place. I remember her awe of being in this exact spot where important ideas reshaped the way nations were ruled.

Both back then with Mom and today with Al, we are at the Acropolis early enough that it feels as if we have the place to ourselves.

Lots of restoration work is going on. Especially at the Parthenon, the largest and most dramatic of the buildings here. At one end, cranes and workers busily restore the huge Ionic columns. Al is spell-bound by the work and the engineering that has gone into this beautiful structure.

The Acropolis' grounds are uneven. I don't see how anyone in a wheelchair can navigate it. The Acropolis earth seems to be a mixture of gravel and marble.

As time passes, more and more people arrive until the place really feels crowded. We can barely move without bumping into someone. The heat increases and the crowds grow, and we decide it's time to go to the shaded gathering place below.

Neither of us wants to take the lift, so we head for the stairs. And I'm thrilled to see that they are very different from when my mother and I were here. Their descent is gentler. The steps themselves are more even than I remember. Al and I make it to the bottom with no problem at all.

By 4 p.m. we're in the Crow's Nest, above the ship's bow. Since our ship is leaving at 4:30 p.m., we want to be here to watch the departure. Hundreds of others have the same idea, so the place is pretty crowded. But still, we can see out the huge windows and watch as we head for our next stop: Istanbul.

An Australian couple comment that they can't believe the lack of upkeep on the buildings in Greece. "People just seem to let things crumble," they say.

I'm sure that others from our ship took tours that included many more sights and many more stops, but Al and I are fully satisfied with what we experienced of Greece: the ancient Plaka, Hadrian's Arch and what's left of Zeus' Temple, and the amazing Acropolis. We'll be talking about this visit for years to come.

When the dinner hour arrives, we head for the dining room. Tonight the ship is serving Greek Moussaka — a hot, eggplant based dish popular in this region of the world. I'm eager to try it.

Along with the moussaka, I order a Moroccon dish that includes apricots and rice.

Al decides on Salmon and onion soup.

My dinner is delicious. The dishes are spicy and tasty.

For dessert, Al chooses sorbet. My meal was so satisfying I skip dessert.

Tonight's show in the theater features Oli Nez, a multi-instrumentalist who combines music and laughter. But we decide to go to the library instead. I choose two books: "Nearing Home," by Billy Graham, and "Growing up Laughing," by Marlo Thomas.

Billy Graham's book is all about growing old and being old, and as I read it in our room, his words comfort me.

As our ship heads toward Istanbul, I take a long, hot bath and wash my hair. Al takes a long hot shower and trims his mustache.

We keep the curtains to our balcony open, and the nearly full moon spreads a wide stream of light across the sea outside.

AL AND THE CONCEPT OF "OLD."

This trip we're on is not just a journey to be measured in miles, but also one to be measured in years; centuries, in fact. As a geezer, I've assumed I know a lot about the passage of time.

For this Californian, "old" means events from the time of the 1849 gold rush. When those eager gold panners arrived dreaming of gleaming treasure, however, the California missions had already been hard at work for nearly a century.

The history of the Europeans who settled the U.S. begins a full century before the Western missions were established, however. That's definitely old to my way of thinking: four centuries of history. Gee! Think of that.

But, in Amsterdam, we learned that the citizens of that lovely city were well into their "golden age" long before Columbus stepped off the ship in the Bahamas.

And that pinnacle of Dutch accomplishment rested on earlier centuries of growth and development. Everywhere we've turned, we find something older. The clear standout in Amsterdam was the Oude Kerk – the Old Church – consecrated in 1306. It was definitely time to readjust my definition of "old."

But when I stepped onto the Acropolis and saw the Parthenon for the first time, I simply could not encompass what I was seeing.

The Parthenon predated the Oude Kerk by 1,744 years.

In the course of traveling from San Francisco to Athens, we'd spanned 6,771 miles and we'd stepped back 2,452 years. Nothing I did – or could have done – prepared me for that.

What's truly amazing – especially to this retired contractor – is that the Parthenon was built by hand. No computers, no power tools, no lasers, no Caterpillar tractors. No plan sets or OSHA or building departments. And once completed, it wasn't simply utilitarian: It was/is endowed with a beauty that utterly transcends two and a half millennia.

I guess that's what ultimately remains with me, perhaps even more than the stunning physical age of the structure. The Parthenon's design is truly timeless.

The Greek civilization, which we deign to call "ancient," clearly treasured design and style and balance. To those long-gone citizens of Athens, there was no separation of art from function: the two were inseparably bound together. And here we are, centuries later, still agape at their work and its timeless beauty.

ARRIVING IN ISTANBUL

One of the views we enjoy during our Bosphorous Strait dinner cruise.

A leisurely breakfast in our sun-filled room. A couple of hours in the Crow's Nest enjoying the scenery as our ship sails through the Dardanelles while the ship's location guide, Tom, describes what we are seeing.

At 10 a.m. we hear a lecture on the ports we'll stop at after Istanbul.

I really like these introductory lectures. Even though I've researched the various ports online and in guidebooks, I always learn something new from the lectures. And the information is up to date, something that's often missing online or in guidebooks.

After the lecture, we take lunch in the lido. Unfortunately, we forgot that we were invited to the Mariner Luncheon today (a perk for folks who have sailed more than once on Holland America).

As our ship approaches Istanbul Harbor in the Bosphorus Strait, the waters grow increasingly crowded. Ships, boats of all sizes and ferries rush in every direction. I've never seen such sea traffic in my life.

AL OBSERVES DOCKING AT ISTANBUL

At Istanbul, our ship docked against the quay (not the pier, you landlubbers). Thanks to the Nieuw Amsterdam's side thrusters, our captain slid the ship into a space not much longer than the vessel.

The question at hand was "How does the captain secure our 87,000-ton ship (and 25,900 tons of overfed passengers) to the dock?" We leaned over the port rail and watched.

When we were within 20 feet (6 meters) and with an unexpectedly loud BANG! Our ship fired small ropes – not much more than clotheslines – toward the dock, each with a monkey's fist (a softball-sized knot of rope) at the end.

Dockworkers grabbed and pulled. The clotheslines were fastened to larger lines. More grabbing and pulling. Then came the huge lines – hawsers, in nautical speak. Industrial-grade grabbing and pulling.

When the ship nestled gently against the quay (impressive ship-handling, if I do say so), those mammoth hawsers were wound around steel bollards (posts) set into the quay, holding the ship firmly in place.

Ta-da.

It was impressive.

✿✿

DINNER ON THE BOSPHORUS

By 3:30 p.m. we are moored. We're right near the mouth of the inlet called the Golden Horn. The weather is beautiful – clear, sunny and warm.

Yesterday we were at the Acropolis – awed by the ruins of the various temples, wowed by the views, trying to take it all in, and here we are this afternoon moored in the harbor at Istanbul, watching so much water traffic bubble by that it reminds us of a crowded freeway at rush hour.

I stand on our balcony, trying to absorb the feel of this ancient city. Istanbul, where Europe and Asia meet. It used to be called Constantinople, named for the Roman Emperor Constantine the Great.

The Byzantine Empire was born here in the fourth century A.D. Later the Ottoman Empire took over. Today it is Turkey's hub for industry and tourism, filled with monuments, historic sites and wonders found nowhere else.

In the background, I can hear the wavering sound of Turkish music. It's so exciting to realize we are really here and we have tonight and almost all day tomorrow to explore.

Among the shore excursions we bought for this trip is a dinner cruise this evening. "A Taste of Istanbul: Dinner Cruise on the Scenic Bosphorus" cost $99.95 each. It should be the perfect introduction to this mysterious megacity.

Al is stretched out on our couch, reading. I'm on our balcony watching all the boats and ferries and police boats and water taxis going every which way in the harbor. The cacophony of waves and boat horns and gulls calling to each other fills the air. I'm loving this chaos.

Dressed for our dinner cruise, we leave the ship at 4:50 p.m. Waiting guides help us climb into a small bus. The bus drives along the harbor for perhaps half a mile. And then we climb off, walk about 50 feet to a double-decker dinner boat.

The water-level deck is enclosed with windows and filled with white-linen- covered round tables. Wine and water glasses are being placed. We're directed to the open top deck, where there are also tables, comfortable chairs and a bar. The warm air and soft evening light surround us. Like many others, Al and I take photos as the boat begins its journey.

169

We cruise past stunning palaces and bulbous mosques with their prickly minarets. On one side of the strait is Europe. On the other, Asia. We're told that Istanbul is the only city in the world to exist in both Europe and Asia.

The others on this dinner cruise are from throughout the world. Three women sitting near us are from Brazil. I hear German being spoken at another table. And an Australian accent at another nearby table.

The conversations are enthusiastic. The cruise commentary is fascinating. We learn the histories of some of the palaces. We learn about the two suspension bridges we'll see this evening: The Bosphorus Bridge and the Fatih Sultan Mehmet Bridge. And we learn that Istanbul is growing so fast, that an accurate count of its population cannot be maintained. The only thing approaching accuracy, according to our cruise host, is to say that Istanbul houses about 16 million residents.

As the sun sets and the air grows chill, we're directed down the steps to the dining room. Although enclosed from the weather, the dining room is all windows, so while we enjoy our dinner, we can also see the passing scenery. Our table mates include a couple from Sacramento, a couple from Canada and a couple from Chicago.

Waiters bring each of us a dinner-sized plate displaying an array of appetizers: dolmas, hummus, an eggplant concoction, a small mound of tuna salad and a fat, flavorful slice of white cheese. Each item is tasty and unusual. I love the various unfamiliar flavors. Exploring new places through food is one of my favorite things.

After appetizers, comes the entree: beef (or is it lamb? Or goat? We at the table think it's beef) wrapped in eggplant, accompanied by rice, peas and carrots.

As we eat and visit, nighttime darkness closes in. The flickering, battery-powered candles on each table create an intimate atmosphere, making faces glow. And outside, city lights illuminate the mosques, palaces, streets and houses along the shores.

I feel Al's hand on my knee and know he's as thrilled with this evening as I am. What could possibly improve this experience? And then we find out.

TURKISH DELIGHT DELIGHTS AL

Dessert: my favorite part of the meal. Any meal, in fact. This is especially so when the entree wanders from tried-and-true I-know-what-I'm-eating fare. Not that something unusual is necessarily bad (the meal on our boat was wonderful, it must be immediately stated), but I'm a creature of habit. In short, now that I've eaten: where's the sweets?

Turkish Delight. *The name conjures up an image of something/someplace exotic; Far Eastern; writhing belly dancers. Swarthy men wearing fezzes and carrying scimitars. A bit over the top, but you get the idea.*

The confection called Turkish Delight was doled out to us, two cubes apiece, each somewhat larger than an inch square (2.5 cm for the metric-minded) and dusted lightly with ... powdered sugar? ... yes.

We nibbled cautiously. Wonderful flavors of fruit and roses danced on our tongues. More chewing. Nuts. All in a gel-gummy texture somewhat like a jelly bean but without the outer shell. Ooooh!

I immediately ate the second piece. Then looked furtively to see if there were thirds or fourths, or what-can-I-smuggle-back-to-the-ship?

✵✵

And to set off our night on the Bosphorus in spectacular fashion, a bright, full moon rises. Al and several other men leave their tables (cameras in hand) and go out on deck to try and capture the night-time beauty.

When he returns, Al says that the two suspension bridges are all lit-up works of art.

"One changes colors," he says. "First all the lights are red, then blue, then yellow. The other bridge you'll just have to see for yourself. It's all dancing lights. I've never seen anything like it. You've got to go out there and see it."

Excusing myself, I step out on deck. Yes, these Istanbul bridges are unforgettable, changing colors and illuminated patterns in the black night with the full moon hovering overhead.

By 10 p.m. the dinner and the river cruise have ended. A bus returns us to the ship. Unfortunately, it drops us off much farther away from our ship than we would like. But we're a large group of happy people, walking home after an unforgettable evening together, so no one complains. And overhead a big, fat, beautiful moon lights our way.

Back in our room, Al and I linger on our balcony. Below us, the dark, choppy waters form a background to scores of seagulls that soar and then settle into the waves and then soar some more. Silent. Beautiful. Poetic. Across the black bay, the lights of Asian Istanbul twinkle. And above it all, the moon sprinkles cool light among the waves.

As we embrace, Al whispers, "It's just magic."

THE BLUE MOSQUE AND THE GRAND BAZAAR

Part of the ceiling in the beautiful, immense Blue Mosque.

Today we have a half-day tour called "Ottoman Wonders." Our bus will leave at 8:30 a.m., so we must be at the theater before that. Off to the lido for breakfast where I get a veggie omelet and Al gets French toast.

There were many Istanbul shore excursions to choose from, but most sounded too exhausting and too expensive.

Our $74.95 half-day tour is full enough. It includes the Blue Mosque (which everyone says is the "must see" for Istanbul), the Topkapi Palace, a carpet weaving demonstration and the Grand Bazaar. We'll also get to see Hagia Sophia but only from a distance. For us, that is a full day.

We're on the bus by 8:20 a.m. Our guide looks like a college student. He speaks excellent English. I think there are about 35 in our tour group. We're group number 3, and we each are given a circular pink nametag bearing a black "3" to stick on our shirt or blouse. Our guide has a large pink, circular paddle with the number 3 on it, which he holds above his head as he leads us on our adventure.

Once we arrive at the Blue Mosque, our first stop this morning, I understand the need for his paddle and our badges. The place is thronged.

One benefit of cruise ship shore excursions is that we don't have to stand in line to get tickets:

entry to the various sites comes automatically with our tour. But as we approach the imposing Blue Mosque with its seven minarets we can see a long, serpentine line. This 17th-century building with its blue tiled domes and pencil sharp minarets along with its courtyards is on a Grand Scale (Capital G, capital S). And the line of people waiting to go inside is equally huge.

Our group falls in line at the end, and slowly we all proceed around the mosque, past the line of faucets — we could call it the men's washroom — where male worshipers wash their heads, hands and arms before entering the mosque. We spend at least a half hour in line, shuffling ever so slowly toward the tourist entrance. As we approach the entrance, our guide points the women to a nearby booth where head coverings are dispensed.

I'm given a light blue cloth. It drapes easily over my head and shoulders. Al snaps a photo. These scarves are not meant to cover our faces, just our hair.

We climb steps and enter a long, covered pavilion with benches where we remove our shoes and slip them into a white, easy-to-carry plastic bag. No one is allowed to enter the mosque wearing shoes. Both the blue scarf for my head and the plastic bag for our shoes are provided free of charge.

And then we enter the mosque. My stockinged feet sink deep into the soft, richly colored carpets. The space inside this building feels immense. It is stunning, majestic and overwhelmingly huge. I feel like an ant. A baby ant. Hundreds, maybe thousands of people stare agape at the walls and domes. Others, like me, snap photos. You can take pictures inside but cannot use the flash on your camera.

Far above us soars the central dome (77-feet / 23.5 meters in diameter and 141 feet/43 meters high), surrounded by eight secondary domes. Their curves are voluptuous.

Soft light streams into this cavernous space through 260 windows, illuminating the 20,000 handmade ceramic tiles that cover all the surfaces of the mosque.

There are chandeliers and lamps and beauty everywhere. Our guide illustrates how people pray here, showing us how they kneel. The Blue Mosque is not only a popular tourist site, it is also a place of worship. Five times a day, worshipers gather here for prayer. During those times, no tourists are allowed inside.

I take many photographs, but the crowds grow and their crush becomes oppressive. I must add that everyone in the mosque – tourists and tour guides and mosque personnel – is patient and polite.

I'm privileged to be here, standing in this stunning 400-year-old place of worship. I doubt I'll ever be here again, so I try to capture it with my camera, my eyes and ears. I want to remember forever what this place feels like.

We're guided out into the courtyard, and on to our next site. A man collects our shoe bags and head coverings.

After the Blue Mosque, which, by the way, was completed within eight years, our group walks past Hagia Sophia, Constantinople's Great Church, which was turned into a mosque and is now a museum, on our way to our next stop, the Topkapi Palace.

I worry about Al's knees, since we're walking more than we expected, but when I ask how he's feeling, he says he's doing fine. This exotic world has captured him.

Topkapi Palace is said to be the largest and oldest palace in the world. It was the primary residence of the Ottoman sultans for about 400 years.

Our guide leads us through the Imperial Gate into the first courtyard. Its size amazes me. The lush green lawns, mature sycamore trees and well-trimmed shrubbery give the place a parklike look. Moms in black burkas keep watch as their toddlers run and play and giggle in the grass.

Our guide hands each of us the ticket we'll need to enter the second courtyard and the various areas of the palace itself. And he points out the cafe where we all need to meet by 1 p.m. I can see that this tour is going to take longer than we thought when we signed up for it. But that's fine. We'll never be here again, and the city is an architectural delight, unlike anything I've ever seen.

As we head for the Gate of Salutation, leading to the second court yard, our guide points out the little Executioner's Fountain, where the executioner washed his hands and blade.

The Gate of Salutation, which is the actual museum entrance, looks like something out of a movie — modeled after medieval European fortresses — with a cylindrical tower on either side of the stone wall containing the gate. We must pass a checkpoint, complete with rifle-toting soldiers, to go through this gate and into the second courtyard.

Again the grassy lawns and manicured shrubbery give an impression of a huge, serene park. This is the courtyard that was used for ceremonial events such as coronations.

Although we don't tour inside the harem complex (it's an additional charge and would take time we don't have), we learn a great deal about the thousands of people who lived here – the sultan and his mother along with his wives, their children and all the concubines and all their children.

This second courtyard also contains the Divan and Divan Tower, the Imperial Treasury's armory and the kitchen complex.

Al and I walk through the Gate of Felicity into the third courtyard. Here we check out the Sultan's Reception Hall, poke our noses into the hall of holy relics and agree that the palace complex is huge and fascinating.

We could easily spend an entire day exploring, but we're running out of energy. The opulent pavilions, jewel-filled treasury, sprawling harem complex and other areas have given us but a glimpse into the life of an exotic and bygone culture.

We make our way back to the cafe, where we'll rest our feet until the tour group arrives.

Despite the crowds, I find a table for two and Al goes to get me a cup of hot chocolate. When he returns he has two small paper cups (about eight ounces each). "No hot chocolate," he says apologetically. "Just coffee."

Turkish coffee. One sip tells me clearly I can't drink this thick, black brew.

Al drains his cup without so much as a wince, and says matter-of-factly, "There's an inch of sludge on the bottom." He adds that he feels revived with a shot of caffeine in his system. Reaching over, he takes my cup and downs its contents, too.

All around us, women wrapped in black burkas and men in long, white robes and golden turbans wander amid crowds of European tourists.

Eventually, our guide leads us all back to the bus, and we take off for our last two stops: a carpet-weaving shop, and the Grand Bazaar. By now it is well into the afternoon. The bus creeps along the traffic-crammed street. I've never been in such a crowded place. From this morning's visit to the Blue Mosque to this afternoon bus ride through the historic town center, we can barely move because of all the other people or all the other vehicles.

Eventually traffic gridlock stops our bus completely. Our guide prepares us for the visit to the carpet shop. He says we'll be shown how the carpets are woven, then we'll be seated and served tea and then the salesmen will display all kinds of carpets hoping we'll buy. He tells us that if we want to buy but don't want to get ripped off we have to haggle. It's all part of the process.

Our bus is going nowhere. The traffic in front of our bus is going nowhere.

So the guide talks about the Grand Bazaar, one of the oldest shopping malls in the world. He says there are 61 covered streets in the market with more than 4,000 shops. He warns us that the mazelike market is filled with pickpockets, so we must be careful.

Our bus has not moved an inch. And our young, energetic guide grows frustrated. We're already well past the time our tour should have ended, and here we sit on a bus going nowhere.

"We'll walk to the carpet shop," he announces. "It isn't far. We'll get there faster on foot."

And off we go. This guide is walking way too fast for us, but he has the pink paddle above his head, so we can keep track of him. The crowds on the sidewalks are as thick as the go-nowhere traffic in the street. Thank goodness someone knows where we're going.

Eventually, we arrive at the Orient Handmade Carpets at Nuruosmaniye Caddesi No. 68 Cagaloglu.

Elegant from the marble floor to the decorative ceiling, this place is impressive. We climb a curving staircase and emerge into a large display room. Once everyone from our group is in the room, the demonstrations begin.

A woman who looks to be about 30 shows us how silkworm cocoons are soaked and carefully unwound, and how the fine silk strands are then wound into threads that can be dyed and woven into carpets.

At a loom, another woman is actually weaving a rug. She has the master design for the rug propped up on top of her loom, and as she weaves one thread at a time through the weft, a man explains what she is doing.

He says that the weavers usually work with only one design. They spend their entire career perfecting their artistry with that design. He says that people in the industry can follow a weaver's professional growth, and can spot an early rug and a latter rug by the improvement in the work.

A weaver may spend a year making one rug. If it's a large one, she may spend more than a year. No wonder these rugs are expensive.

The man who is explaining everything talks about the natural, organic dyes, and the more current, chemical dyes. He talks about the various designs, and just about the time that all this information is beginning to feel like overload, the lecture and carpet-making demonstration ends.

And we are led to a large room where padded seats line the walls. Once seated, young men bearing silver trays filled with steaming cups serve us hot apple tea. Other young men follow, with baskets of freshly made pretzels.

And the sales pitch begins.

Rug after drop-dead gorgeous rug is unrolled on the floor in front of us. Four muscular young men roll them out as a suited salesman describes each rug's virtues. The men roll out huge rugs that would fill ballrooms, and smaller ones that would fill living rooms or bedrooms. Reds and blues and purples. Floral designs and stylistic animals and geometric displays. The colors are vibrant and the carpets unbelievably beautiful.

The salesman describes the difference between wool and silk carpets, and illustrates how the silk changes color as the light hits it from different angles.

Rug after rug unrolls in dazzling splendor. The floor is covered in textile art so intense you have to squint. Some rugs are so stunning that we gasp or sigh as a group when they're unfurled. No wonder Turkish rugs are so sought-after, so famous.

"Let's get a rug," Al says.

"Are you crazy?" I whisper, my Scottish soul shriveling at the thought of spending thousands on a carpet I wouldn't want anyone to step on.

An observant salesman approaches and asks if there's something he can show us. Al says we'd like to see smaller rugs with a lot of blue (my favorite color). And before I know it, dark-eyed young men are unrolling carpet after carpet with blue backgrounds, blue designs, blue this, blue that.

One rug, about five by seven feet, with cream-colored fringe and elegant floral designs, captures my attention. Al is smiling at me with big, eager eyes. The salesman approaches with his smart phone.

"How much?" I ask.

He says, "five-thousand."

I say, "Dollars?" and immediately think of all the ways I could spend five thousand dollars. My Scottish ancestors are already squirming in their graves.

He nods, "Yes."

I say, "No."

He starts explaining why it is worth that much money.

"It may be worth that much, but we don't have that much to spend," I say, and begin to walk away.

He quickly refigures the cost using his smartphone, and says he can sell it to us for $4,000.

I say, "No."

He goes down to $3,500. And we continue haggling. I don't like haggling. It makes me uncomfortable. But I also try to be careful with money. We are retired, after all, and in the current United States' economy, our investments are earning virtually no interest. So while this may be a fun game to the salesman or other shoppers, I am serious about not spending more than we can afford.

He shows me the word "Hereke" woven into a corner of the carpet and says Hereke has been at the leading edge of handmade carpet production since 1843. He says a Hereke carpet is the finest hand made carpet in the world.

We continue to haggle and eventually reach a price that sounds somewhat reasonable (to my uneducated ears). It's still expensive but I see that Sweetheart's eyes continue to shine. He whispers,

"It's a beautiful investment. It will most likely increase in value."

"O. K.," I say.

Al says, "We'll buy it."

Al takes care of the paperwork details.

I don't know if we've made a good deal or paid more than we should have. But back home we'll have this glorious carpet to hang on a wall, and we'll remember how it was made by hand, and we'll recall hot apple tea and fresh-baked pretzels, and a lovely afternoon in Istanbul.

Then it's off to the Grand Bazaar.

Since our bus is still sitting at a gridlocked intersection, we follow our guide on foot to the Grand Bazaar.

The crowds on the sidewalk are so thick they flow out onto the street, where traffic remains at a standstill. We cannot walk without bumping into other people or having other people bump into us. I can see how easy it would be to pick pockets in crowds like this. Luckily Al wears a money belt, and I have a little secure pouch hanging from around my neck. It holds my digital camera, my room key, my passport, some cash and a credit card. And it hangs in front, so no one's going to be able to slip anything out of it.

I wonder what would it be like to grow up in such a teeming city? Would claustrophobia be your constant companion? Or would you be so used to the crush of crowds that you'd feel frightened if left alone? I can't imagine living in this kind of swarm day after day. I think I'd feel suffocated.

As we approach the bazaar, the crowds increase. And I feel squeezed and pressed, like an olive being turned into oil. As we enter the huge, covered main street, the crowd thins a little and we stand there, dazzled.

There are shops selling leather, jewelry, shoes, lamps, spices, silk, candy, books, art, sculptures, dolls and antiques, carpets and calligraphy, food, hand-painted ceramics, clothes, guitars and mandolins and other musical instruments, textiles and games like backgammon, tulip-shaped tea glasses and ... you name it, you can find it in the Grand Bazaar.

Everywhere people are buying or selling or just looking. The place is a frenzy of lights and colors. It's astounding. It's overwhelming.

Al pulls me into a candy shop to point out shelf after shelf of boxed Turkish Delight. There are many different flavors, with and without nuts. Something for every palate. And before we leave, Sweetheart has five boxes of the confection under his arm. Some of them are for gifts, he insists. Time will tell if there's anything left to give away by the time we get back to California.

The Grand Bazaar deserves much more time and attention than we have on this tour. When our group eventually makes it back to the bus, we discover it has moved to a nearby parking lot. Our guide and all the rest of us climb aboard.

When the bus driver slides into his seat, we notice a problem. The parking lot is crammed. Cars and trucks and shuttles and tour buses face in all directions. There is no way out. No one can move.

Our guide, clearly frustrated beyond belief, takes off somewhere and returns with half a dozen men who start aggressively directing traffic. Little by little, with plenty of shouting and gesturing, they get vehicles to back up a few inches, then squeeze over a bit, then turn out and eventually, after maybe half an hour of minute moves, finally pull out of the lot.

Our bus is the third vehicle to make it out onto the main thoroughfare.

We're back onboard ship by 4 p.m. Our tour grew from four to eight-hours. And it was wonderful. Last night's cruise and today's walking tour have given us a fabulous sampling of this ancient and exotic city.

By 5:30 p.m. the ship is on its way again, and we're enjoying dinner at Canaletto. This is one of the onboard specialty restaurants. Specialty restaurants charge for their meals, from $10 to $45. We rarely take advantage of them, since we find the food in the lido or the main restaurant, the Manhattan Dining Room, to be excellent. But, this dinner is a gift from our travel agent, and we're happy to enjoy the quiet, ocean view as we dine. We order small plates to share.

Our first course includes fisherman's stew (mussels, shrimp, clams, scallops and chunks of fish). Delicious. Also caponata, an eggplant mixture with golden raisins and pine nuts, served on little toasted rounds of bread. Equally tasty.

Our second course: ravioli with leeks and sun-dried tomatoes.

Chicken cacciatori on a bed of polenta is our third course. The chicken thighs are so tender the meat voluntarily drops from the bone. Every dish is a tastebud's delight.

For dessert: gelato. Al has strawberry. I have chocolate. Each comes with a sliver of cinnamon cookie.

By the end of dinner, we're so tired (and sore) from our day of walking, that we simply return to our room for the night. I take a long, hot bath. Al takes a long, hot shower. And we climb into bed with our books. Soon, we turn off the lights.

Thursday, Oct. 9

LESBOS, GREECE

The Church of Agios Therapon towers over the fishing village of Mytilene on the Greek island of Lesbos.

When we awaken, our ship is meandering toward the Greek Island of Lesbos. We'll anchor from 11 a.m. to 6 p.m. at Mytilene, the capital and port of this island.

After breakfast in the dining room — lox and bagels for Al, corned beef hash and eggs for me — we're off to the library. Al is on his fourth novel.

We find a windowside table for two, and settle in. The morning sun has turned the gentle waters a warm blue. Emerald hills with white-washed beach villages pass slowly under a pale azure sky.

While we read, the espresso machine's whine and fizz fills the background, and people study the little snacks under glass at the espresso counter: coffeecake, muffins, croissants, fruit cups.

Soon our ship maneuvers offshore and the crew readies today's tenders. When a harbor is not deep enough for a ship to anchor at a pier, the ship anchors farther out, and small boats called tenders ferry us between ship and shore. Today, all those going ashore will board tenders.

By 11 a.m. we're back in our room. The ship lays quietly, 46 tons of chain and anchor holding it in place.

A phone call from Percell suggests we meet in the Showroom and go see Mytilene together. Perfect idea.

When the four of us climb out of the tender, we're directed through a long, fully fenced parking lot that leads us to one of the harbor sidewalks. This is the way we must go to reach the main streets of Mytilene.

As we walk along chatting, I notice people sitting around the parked cars. Lots of people. At first I think they might be kids with skateboards, but as I take closer note I see they are older than kids. They are families. Fathers, mothers, children of all ages, infants.

Some lean against parked cars. Some of the women are nursing babies. They resemble displaced people, the kind we see back home on the evening news.

Tina and I look at each other in shock.

"What do you think?" I ask. "Refugees? Asylum seekers?"

She nods "Yes."

I can't imagine living in a parking lot, trying to care for babes and toddlers while living on asphalt, no shelter or shade. We try not to stare.

As we leave the fenced parking lot, Tina asks a man who looks as if he's in charge, if all those people are refugees. He says they are. From Syria. And he points out some nearby mobile structures that have been set up to serve them. One is clearly a medical clinic. We can't tell what the others are used for. But it is obvious these people – and it looks like there are hundreds of them – now call a parking lot "home." The reality of their suffering and our inability to do anything about it dampens our spirits.

Here we are, the four of us, on the cruise of a lifetime while hundreds of others have fled their homes and now live in a Mytilene parking lot. Life is such a jumble. And there are times like this when you feel painfully helpless.

As we stroll along the harbor, heading for town, we're amazed by the huge domed church looming above all the other buildings. While Tina and Al shoot pictures of the many boats and yachts tied up in the harbor, Percell and I stare at the church. It dwarfs the rest of the town. That is the building we want to see.

A gentle breeze stirs the harbor, snapping lines against metal masts with a click-click sound.

The closer we get to town, the larger the church grows. And as we reach the beautiful building of the Lesbos Prefecture, right in the middle of town, we find ourselves suddenly swallowed by an agitated crowd.

At first it feels like a celebration, but the feeling quickly changes to something more like an angry protest. Like something I don't want to be part of. Uniformed police are pushing people. Men are shouting.

Al, Percell and Tina catch the same sense I have, and the four of us grab hands and try to stay together as we hurry through the growing, chattering crowd.

In front of the building with its huge white columns, we come upon a slaughtered goat and parts of other dead goats strewn about on the sidewalk. The stench is horrible. The site, bathed in blood, is frightening. Obviously, something very unpleasant is going on here.

As quickly as we can, we squeeze out of the crowd and head purposefully toward the bulbous dome of the huge church.

Within minutes we're on a busy little street full of pedestrians and motor scooters. No more bloody goat bodies, no more angry crowds, just shops – book shops, antique shops, handmade ceramics and jewelry shops. We come upon a fish market where we could buy sardines, millet, octopus or more.

The morning heat grows and I hope we can find the entrance to the big church. We turn a corner, walk up a graffiti-laden side street, turn right and find ourselves in the courtyard of the Church of Agios Therapon. This majestic basilica has five towering domes and two tiers of columns – Ionic and Corinthian. And the building is just beautiful. A plaque says it was built at the beginning of the 19th century.

Once inside, the cool, quiet air refreshes me.

The ornate interior boasts a huge chandelier and intricately carved wooden seats rather than pews. The place is breathtaking inside and out. We spend a lot of time there with our cameras snapping.

And eventually the four of us go back outside and sit together on a bench, to simply stare at this magnificent building and let its beauty sink in.

Yet, this place of elegant beauty is surrounded by graffiti-filled walls. Maybe the citizens of Mytilene don't consider graffiti a blot on the neighborhood.

Our growling stomachs send us back to the harbor, where there are many seaside restaurants and cafes.

We find what looks like a great place. I love the colors of the wooden tables and chairs – greens and yellows and blues. The people speak little English (which Tina and I think is a good sign). We order cheese-and-eggplant-stuffed peppers. Fried squid. Various vegetable dishes. I get a small plate of spaghetti with vegetables and we all enjoy a long and lovely lunch.

After lunch Tina and Percell decide to do some shopping.

Al and I mosey along the harbor, stopping often to take pictures of the fishing boats moored at the docks, or the anchored sailboats easily riding the gentle swells. Eventually we return to the refugee-filled parking lot and catch a tender home.

Mytilene is smaller and quieter than other ports we've visited. But I like that. There are things to do here and places to see that we missed because we focused on the church and on a long lunch together.

Yet even here, in this idyllic spot, the problems of the world are evident. While the poor asylum-seekers in the parking lot are probably grateful to have reached safety on the island of Lesbos, now what? Where can they go to rebuild their war-shattered lives?

✴✴

By 6:30 p.m. our ship steams away from Lesbos and toward Ephesus. The sun has slipped behind the hills, leaving the sky aglow. A few stalwart seagulls glide alongside our ship.

After dinner Al and I go to the Explorer's Lounge (one of the many lounges and bars providing live music) to listen to the duo, Adagio, play classical pieces. Adagio consists of a pianist and a violinist. Two lovely and talented women playing beautiful and sophisticated classical music.

I love the fact that this ship offers so much live music. Nearly every bar and lounge has live music in the evening. When so much of today's music is recorded, it's refreshingly wonderful to listen and watch musicians create cool jazz and hot rock, listen to familiar melodies from the American songbook, or hear a little toe-tappin' country. Tonight's brief concert of classical greats is perfect after a day on Lesbos that was both radiant and disturbing.

By 8 p.m. we're in the Showroom, ready to enjoy Pianist Elliot Finkel. When he strides out on stage, we see what a large man he is. Way taller than six feet, and as broad as a football lineman, it's obvious that he relishes the spotlight. And as the evening progresses, I like him more and more. He plays pieces by Gershwin, Schubert and others. He tells jokes. And family stories.

It turns out he's the son of Fyvush Finkel, an actor who played Douglas Wambaugh on the television show "Picket Fences." I remember his dad in that role and how much I liked the character he portrayed. Elliot's family stories draw me in and make me feel like I'm almost a family friend.

His energy seems endless. He plays the grand piano intensely and energetically, and even before he's finishes a piece, he turns to the audience as if to say, "Isn't this fun!" I admit it is.

Friday, Oct. 10

EPHESUS, TURKEY

Ephesus' Celsus Library (facade shown here) was one of the largest libraries of the ancient world.

We will be in port today from 7 a.m. to 4 p.m. And, like yesterday, we'll ride a tender to shore. Today's tour (our last shore excursion) is entitled

"Ancient Ephesus & the Virgin Mary's House," and cost $84.95. It starts promptly at 8 a.m.

The day is sunny and warm. We ride past cotton fields and olive and fig orchards while our guide explains some of the history and geography of the area.

The bus climbs about 2,000 feet to the hillside of Mount Koressos where the Virgin Mary's house stands, awaiting its daily arrival of tourists.

From the parking lot we walk a long, gently rising paved path to Mary's house. The day is young, the olive-tree-lined path leads through beautiful gardens. And when we see the one-story stone house, we feel that we're on holy ground.

There's a tiny amphitheater beside the house where priests hold Mass. But our guide says only about 30 people attend. "There are almost no Christians in Turkey," she says.

I assume the amphitheater seats are filled with tourists on Sundays.

Legend has it that this is where the mother of Jesus spent her final years. It is where (according to Catholic doctrine) she ascended to heaven. This tranquil spot fills me with peace. And I can hope that, after the agony of seeing her son tortured to death, she actually found such a serene spot to spend her final years.

Soon we are inside the modest stone dwelling where silence is observed. We walk through three rooms. One was Mary's bedroom. The ceilings are vaulted. Pope John Paul II's chalice and stole, from when he visited this shrine in 1979, are on display, along with pictures and icons. Within minutes, we're back outside.

There is a counter-high shelf with sand-filled pockets nearby where people can light slim white candles and stand them upright in the sand. Each of us adds our own candle to the glowing collection.

As we start down the paved path heading back to the parking lot, we pass a lengthy stone wall bearing thousands of paper notes – prayers and requests. The notes, fastened to the side of the wall, fill an area about six feet tall that stretches on for yards. All the yearnings, all the gratitude, all the tears that those small slips of paper symbolize, silence the touristy chatter and all of us walk quietly back to our buses.

Our next stop is ancient Ephesus. Although the description said that this tour includes lots of walking, we couldn't dare miss Ephesus. Originally a Greek city, during the Roman Empire it was the second largest city of the realm. The largest was, of course, Rome.

In those heady days of ancient Ephesus, its harbor bustled with trade. The rich and famous built homes here, or visited often. St. Paul conducted missionary work here and wrote his first Epistle to the Corinthians here. Al and I have been looking forward to visiting this place.

The sun is high and the air hot when our walking tour of Ephesus begins. Each of us receives an ear piece and a receiver on a ribbon to wear around our neck. This way, we can clearly hear our guide describing the various things we see, no matter how far away from us she is.

Our guide, a woman who speaks flawless English, says she was a lawyer who specialized in translations. She carries a colorful umbrella that helps us spot her amid the crowds. And there are definitely crowds here.

Although the once-thriving city is now in ruins, the marble bones tell marvelous stories. We see elegant carvings and dramatic columns and streets and courtyards paved in mosaic tiles. We see the remnants of baths and public toilets.

And everywhere among the ruins are sweet, plump cats ... stretching out in the sun on slabs of ancient marble, or grooming themselves atop marble posts or broken marble columns or posing like professional models. They seem totally comfortable with the crowds and our cameras.

Our guide says the cats are encouraged to live here because they keep rodents away.

The most stunning structure is the Library of Celsus, brightly gilded in the midday sunshine. This resplendent structure was the third largest library of the ancient world. Its two soaring stories stand atop a steep set of stairs. And by the time we reach it, hundreds of others are swarming the stairs, standing in the doorways, shooting pictures this way and that. We are just like all the others, eager to capture the beauty and wonder of this place with our cameras.

We climb the steep stone stairs and shoot photos of everything we see. We're dazzled by the radiance and wonder of it all.

Aside from the dramatic library, what most impresses me is Harbor Street — a broad, long avenue of marble with columns, like sentinels, standing along both sides. Our guide says that Cleopatra and Mark Anthony strolled this avenue on their honeymoon, bringing papyrus scrolls as gifts to the Ephesus library. In those days, fountains, arches and shops lined the broad, paved street. I love the thought (and the reality) that I'm walking where Cleopatra once walked, perhaps even stepping in her footprints.

As we continue, we pass the great, hillside theater where St. Paul once preached. The theater could seat about 20,000, and the acoustics were so good that everyone could hear him.

Eventually we make it back to the bus. Al and I and our knees are more than ready to sit and be driven back to the harbor.

On our ride back, we catch a glimpse of the jail where St. Paul was held prisoner.

Although we're dropped off at the ship, we find a harborside cafe with free Wi-Fi and decide it's time to connect with the rest of the world.

First, however, we order chocolate ice cream, but the place is out of chocolate. So we order pistachio. The waiter says, somewhat bashfully, that there's only enough for one serving, so we finish the cafe's pistachio and share the one serving – green ice cream with chocolate syrup. Perfect for a hot afternoon in Turkey!

Al sends a message to his good friend, photographer Bill Jackson. I send messages to my sister and brother.

We've been pleasantly surprised at how easy it is to find cafes and restaurants with Internet connections.

Our table overlooks the water, glittering in the sunshine. Staring at the clear, blue-green liquid, I can see fish, both large and little, swimming around just below us. Above, huge clouds of white gulls circle in the afternoon blue and then settle at the end of this pier.

At a nearby table, a woman talks by Skype with her daughter, telling all about the cruise and showing her the beautiful setting here with the water and the houses climbing the hill behind us.

Another woman, blonde hair pulled back with a black band, deals with two toddlers who are enthusiastically eating ice cream. The afternoon breeze refreshes me.

I love watching the fish and the cloud of white gulls and thinking about the marble buildings and grand monuments of Ephesus.

When we finally return to our room, we find an invitation waiting in our mailbox. It is to enjoy an after-dinner drink with the captain tonight from 7:30 to 8:15 in the Crow's Nest. We'll be there.

We love the soft evening light as our ship pulls away from the pier and heads out into the Aegean Sea, heading for the Greek isle of Santorini.

But first, it's dinner time. At the Manhattan Dining Room, we ask for a table for two. After this amazing day, we don't feel like socializing but want to just eat and think.

Al has rack of lamb.

I have pad Thai with soft-shelled crab. I'm disappointed in my choice. The crab is deep-fried. The pad Thai too spicy for me.

I make up for it with an excellent crème brulee dessert.

And then we're off to the Crow's Nest and the captains cocktail party. We and about 200 others.

As we enter the Crow's Nest, the entire captain's staff greets us – it's like a reception line, shaking hands and saying something pleasant. We're pleased to find plenty of beautiful glasses full of nonalcoholic fruit punch. And circulating throughout the room are tray-carrying waiters, offering lovely hors d'oeuvres.

After eight days onboard, I see lots of familiar faces. These are people I've seen around the ship or on our shore excursion. Although I don't know their names, I feel at home with them, and strike up conversations with a number. It's nice to feel at ease with others who are sharing this wonderful cruise.

Then Al and I head to the Showroom theater for tonight's entertainment – magician and comedian John Lenahan. I haven't laughed so hard in years.

Although we don't always attend the nightly shows in the Showroom theater, when we do, we're usually pleased.

Some of our friends back home have complained about the quality of cruise ship entertainers, but I've always found them entertaining. And I'm amazed at the variety of performers — from music to magic to comedy, to ... well, you name it. Every night there's something new.

And these entertainers are playing for an audience filled with people who may have saved for years to take this trip. I'm sure that adds some pressure to their performance.

All I can say about John Lenahan is that he was hilarious!

✦✦

After a fabulous day amid ruins of past empires, it is going to sound so shallow and pathetic to complain about what's on the TV in our room. But that's what I'm about to do.

Our TV is a flat-screen, wall-mounted affair. It carries channels that show our ship's position, describe what's for sale in ship shops (liquor, watches, clothing, jewelry, bags and lots of other stuff), two news channels: Fox and NBC, three movie channels and two ESPN channels.

I keep hoping to see some of the baseball play-off games. I'm a San Francisco Giants fan and long to catch one of their games. But no such luck.

There are cricket games and soccer tournaments — once we even saw a curling competition — but no American baseball or football.

THE INSIDE SCOOP ON SHORE EXCURSIONS

Half the fun of taking a cruise is exploring new places. Places we're unlikely to visit on our own. But the expense of shore excursions can add significantly to the cost of a cruise. If you're anything like me, you want to spend your precious dollars wisely.

When the ship docks, we have three choices: stay onboard, go on a shore excursion or go ashore and explore on our own.

Al and I often explore on our own, taking our cameras and simply seeing what catches our fancy. I like this kind of exploring because it makes me feel like a kid again. We have also hired a local taxi to visit just one or two sites that are of particular interest, which we checked out online before the cruise.

On the other hand, shore excursions offer a convenient, hassle-free way to see famous or fascinating sites, and they make the most efficient use of our limited time ashore.

The array of cruise ship tours can be mind-boggling – from half-day to full-day tours, bus tours, walking tours, shopping tours, highly active tours that include zip lines or bicycle rides, snorkeling or other activities.

If you want to spend your vacation funds wisely, you'll need to do some research, figure out what interests you most, and study what the various tours offer.

Irene Gruenwald, shore excursion manager on our ship, agrees to share a little insight about shore excursions.

The first thing she says is that a shore excursion is a condensed tour. "The guide has four hours, or perhaps one day, to introduce you to the highlights of their city. And they want you to be happy with what you see and do."

She makes it clear, however, that the guide is on a schedule, and has to keep the group organized and moving along.

If Percell and Tina and Al and I had been on tour in Mytilene, we most likely would not have been able to take our time in the Church of Agios Therapon. We would not have been able to enjoy a leisurely lunch in the little seaside restaurant. And spend the afternoon shopping or photographing.

On the other hand, we would have seen more sites – like the Archaeological Museum, the Teriade Museum, and other churches and museums.

When I ask Irene the benefits of a shore excursion versus exploring on our own, she points out a number of advantages.

"Cruise line shore excursions offer a kind of protection," she says. "We have vetted the tour operators. They must be established, with a good reputation. They must carry insurance. There are lots of hoops they have to jump through.

"On a cruise shore excursion, you know you are safe, you know you'll be returned to the ship on time. And if anything bad happens, like you fall and break your arm, you are covered by insurance."

She also points out that when a passenger buys a shore excursion, it comes with transportation to and from the ship, a guide well-versed on the sites to be seen and includes tickets to any museum, monument or other place on the tour that charges entrance fees.

"So you don't have to wait in a ticket line that might be half an hour long," she says. "It's all taken care of for you. We do it all."

I ask if she has any secrets for choosing the perfect shore excursion.

"Know what's important to you. Home in on what you've always dreamed of. Pre-book if possible," she says.

"You would be surprised at the number of people who have no idea what they most want to see or experience. Since you will only have one day in port, it's unlikely you'll be able to see or do everything. So think about what you most want to see. Prioritize. Then study the offerings."

In the shore excursion catalog in our cabin, each tour description includes an activity-level rating, from easy to strenuous. I mention how much Al and I appreciate such information.

"Yes, you have to take into account your own abilities," she says. "We don't want our guests so worn out at the end of the cruise that they have to take a vacation to recover. It's important, no matter what your age, to learn to pace yourself."

Perhaps the most important point Irene makes is that "You don't have to buy a tour in every port."

On this 12-day cruise to a part of the world we may never see again, Al and I have bought four shore excursions: In Greece, Athens and the Acropolis; In Istanbul, the dinner cruise and, the next day, the Ottoman Empire tour; and in Turkey, Ancient Ephesus and the Virgin Mary's House tour.

On these tours we saw things we probably would not have been able to see on our own. And these were things we really wanted to see and experience.

However, these tours added $679 to the cost of our cruise. Other tours could have added thousands. We are pleased with the value we received. But it's important to know what you can afford and what gives you the best value for your money.

We're enjoying our stops at other ports by exploring on our own, or with Percell and Tina.

As Irene points out, there is no need to buy a tour at every port. We love exploring on our own, and getting the feel of the place without being part of a tourist crowd.

You can research in-port activities on line before you ever step aboard a cruise ship by going to your cruise line's list of shore excursions.

And you can see what other cruisers think about the excursions you might like to take, by going to the website: cruisecritic.com

Saturday, Oct. 11

SANTORINI, GREECE

The Greek island of Santorini is one of the most beautiful places
we visited.

Today we visit the most beautiful of the Greek
islands. At least in my estimation.

Many years ago my mother and I wandered the streets of Fira, the main town on this island, mesmerized by the beauty of the place – all angles and curves of white, topped by domes, the whole place encircled by a deep blue bay.

On that visit, we rode donkeys up the steep switchback road to the top. One such ride was enough for me. I felt sorry for the poor donkeys. And I felt sorry for my poor bottom and back.

And since there's absolutely no way Al and I can make it up or down the road stretching from beach to clifftop, we'll no doubt take the cable car.

Here's a fact that confuses me, and may amuse you. When I was in my 20s, I spent many a weekend sky diving. I loved jumping out of little Cessna 152s, and floating under a canopy to the earth far below.

Since passing 60, however, I've grown frightened by cable cars and other height-spanning contraptions. So the three-minute ride today from the beach to the top of the cliff (and the top of the cliff back down to the beach) is going to be a challenge for me. But I think it's a challenge I can handle, considering that I survived the Acropolis lift without screaming or passing out.

AL IN SANTORINI

All I knew about Santorini was that it had white buildings with blue domes. I'd seen pictures in travel brochures and I'd heard the shore excursion spiel.

Sunny has been enthusiastic about Santorini, telling me how much my camera lens will love the place. And her enthusiasm is often contagious.

This morning I gazed across the ship's deck at our destination as we dropped anchor and unloaded tenders. There, across the harbor, a sheer cliff rose, hundreds of feet high, on top of which was a gaggle of little sugar-cube buildings ... like a thick coating of clumpy frosting.

A path/road zigzagged its way up the cliff, dotted with moving specks I assumed were humans. We had been told during the shore excursion spiel that the summit could be reached on foot (587 steep steps: I don't think so) or on mule-back (ditto). But there was a cable car, which I couldn't see from the ship. That sounded good to me.

In short order, a goodly number boarded the bobbing tender and headed for shore. Many faces were turning a lovely pale green by the time we arrived.

"Shore" was little more than a base-of-cliff shelf with stuff-for-tourist stores and a few cafes.

Many of the herd turned right and headed for the zigzag road. "Where's the mules, Dorothy?" The rest of us smugly turned left and went for the cable car, euros in hand.

Having survived the Acropolis elevator, I felt I knew something about vertical lifts of dubious character. I was not to be disappointed in Santorini.

Santorini's cable car is somewhat like one of those classic two-pulley clotheslines – you know, the one your grandmother had outside her third-floor apartment window, grandpa's underwear drying far above the alley below.

Or perhaps a better analogy is an enclosed ski lift. Riders climb into tiny fully enclosed cabs, four to six per cab, just like flying coach, but without the salty snack. And just like gramma's clothesline writ large, a truly impressive wire rope winds its way around two mammoth steel pulleys – one at the bottom of the lift, the second at the top. Each cab clings to the cable with an arm like a sort of steel clothespin.

Engineer alert: The cable car system runs in one direction (clockwise, viewed from below, to be specific). Cabs go down the right side and back up the left. The vertical lift has to be nearly 600 feet at a pitch of 60 to 70 degrees. Idler pulleys mounted on concrete pylons (how did they ever pour the concrete?) poke out of the cliff face like rocky cactuses, keeping the wire rope from drooping. I was impressed.

The system runs continuously, with stops for loading and unloading being brief. There's no time to contemplate your fate. It's get in, sit down, and No Screaming. I barely had time to look around for an icon of St. Irene (Santorini is a contraction of her name) before we headed down and wound around the bottom pulley. From there, it was straight up. Quickly. "Houston we have lift-off!!"

Our lift-mates closed their eyes, some surely contemplating walking back down. If they survived going up, that is.

Austrian-built, the cable car gave us an incredibly smooth three-minute ride. As we climbed, the view grew ever more spectacular. The Nieuw Amsterdam floated in the middle of a deep blue lagoon, which I recognized as a caldera from a long-ago volcanic eruption.

The sky was deep blue, too, with fluffy white clouds. We could not have asked for a better day.

To a mix of amazement and applause, we topped the lift, spun around the upper pulley and quickly clambered out of our cab. "Thank you for flying Santorini Airlines!" We had arrived! Fira, here we come!

My usual strategy is to go left (did you know research shows that humans circle counterclockwise in a crisis?), and so we did, up a narrow cobblestone walk with stone walls on both sides.

Looking up, we saw white spires and a blue and gold dome with a cross. It had to be a church. A bell tower stood to the side, white and blue, three bells below, one above, a cross on the top. My kind of place. We headed for it.

What Sunny and I found was the Roman Catholic cathedral. Since Greece is Orthodox, I was surprised by our find. The cathedral was – is, should you ever visit – a little gem: filled with history, light and welcoming.

A small crowd gathered at the side altar, and a priest – Greek – came out of the sacristy in robes. It was time for morning Mass. I stayed for the service while Sunny went exploring.

I didn't understand a word that was being said (and I wasn't alone), but the service followed the same order my home parish in California follows, so I made my responses in English and no one seemed to mind. Mass ended, Sunny was waiting by the door, we took many pictures of the cathedral inside and out, and we headed up toward the north end of town.

At the far northern end of Fira – well beyond a parking lot and some rocky ruins and outside usual tourist range – we discovered a little white chapel (closed, unfortunately) that was our second gem-of-the-day. Its rounded dome was the stuff of guidebooks and postcards. We took a lot more pictures and slowly walked back toward the town center. It was time for a bite to eat, ideally one with free Wi-Fi. I felt the need to check email.

Returning to the place we left the lift, we found the rest of our ship's contingent, all congratulating themselves at having made the ascent up the cliff by foot or by mule. Both groups urgently needed showers.

Quickly moving on, we found ourselves at the corner of Mapkoy and Nomikoy Streets where we spotted the Estioporo Cafe (free Wi-Fi) included. It was time to sit down and give our feet and knees a rest.

The Estioporo is a small, family-run establishment with a welcoming patio, shaded for protection from the sun. It was, of course, painted in white and blue. The menu offered what we'd come to expect in Greece: lamb, octopus and eggplant. We thought we'd try lighter fare: perhaps dessert? We're on vacation! How about the baklava?

If you're not familiar with this confection, baklava's an assemblage of phyllo dough infused with honey and packed with bits of nuts. The baklava we get at home in California is good. It usually comes in small squares about the size of a high school bake sale's brownies. A nice munch to round off a meal, nothing more. Based on our experience, we ordered one baklava apiece: enough to tide us over until we got back to the ship.

When our order arrived, we could barely speak. Surely our wide eyes and wide smiles told the waitress we were surprised. The Estioporo's baklava was not a dinky little square. No! It was a quarter-of-a-pie-shaped chunk that stood nearly three inches tall. The phyllo dough had been baked to such a level of flaky perfection that only the honey kept it from being blown away on the gentle afternoon breeze. I could imagine the days (or weeks) of work the bees had put in to make that much honey, and the nuts ... well ... what can I say?

Once we'd recovered from the surprise and had taken several pictures, we set to work with our forks. It was more than the two of us could eat, but we couldn't let it go to waste, so we soldiered on.

Sunny finally gave up. I finished mine and hers, too. Call a cab and take me home. I'm ready for a nap. That not being possible, I emailed and, eventually, waddled happily back onto the street.

Taking our time, we crossed a ridge and dropped down to the far side of the town, then headed south. That area of Fira was more urban Europe than the guidebook area we'd seen earlier: stores, traffic, crowds of locals and tourists.

It was there that we found a small park with a monument recognizing the "Greek Genocide," of which we knew nothing. A sobering explanation described the massacre of 350,000 Greek Christians in what is now northern Turkey, in the years 1914-1923. A sad testimony, and a sad reminder that nothing much has changed.

"When will they ever learn? When will they ever learn?"

Moving on, we went back uphill, discovering the Greek Orthodox cathedral. It was a beautiful white building with a long, shaded portico, facing the harbor. Unlike at the Catholic cathedral, we weren't allowed to take pictures inside. Nearby was the Museum of Prehistoric Thira. We looked around and turned back toward the cable car landing. Santorini was lovely, but my knees and back were done for the day.

And thus back to the cable car, a breath taking descent to the beach, and a bouncing tender ride back to the ship. We returned with hearts full of memories and cameras full of images.

Lunch beckoned, as did some time flat on our bed. How I hope we can make it back someday to this beautiful island!

Following lunch onboard (pork loin and rice for Al, curried lamb for me) we spend an easygoing afternoon napping, reading and looking through the wonderful photos we've taken.

Al says, "You can't take an ugly shot on Santorini." And he's right. All the lines are clean and sharp. Whites and blues and pinks and goldens. The light sets the soft shades aglow. We caught some of that grace and beauty with our cameras. So we'll be taking it home with us. How lucky is that!

At 4 p.m., I go to the Screening Room (the onboard movie theater) to watch "Mama Mia." Released in 2008, this musical romantic comedy is set on a Greek island. It stars Meryl Streep, Pierce Brosnan, Colin Firth, Christine Baranski and Stellan Skarsgard, among others.

But the biggest star of the movie is ABBA's wonderful music. Among the movie's songs: "Fernando," "Money, Money, Money," "Mamma Mia," "Dancing Queen," "The Winner Takes It All," and "Take a Chance on Me."

The Screening Room has about 30 big, comfy chairs, and free popcorn.

This movie with its memorable music and fluffy theme is just perfect after a day meandering the picturesque streets of a Greek island.

Sunday, Oct. 12

ARGOSTOLI, GREECE

We share a tasty salad on Argostoli.

Today's our last port stop before we dock back in Venice. Up by 7:30 a.m., we watch green Greek isles glide past as we dress. The sun sprinkles a wide path of bright glitter across the mackerel sea. We should arrive in Argostoli by noon. I can't get over how quickly this cruise is drawing to a close.

We head for breakfast in the dining room. As we are being seated, I see Tina and Percell enter, and give them a wave. They join us. And our conversation is lively.

I tell them how I was scared to death riding the cable car down from Fira yesterday. I'd read in a guidebook that the cable car system can handle only 36 people at a time.

After Al and I climbed into our little cable car, two excessively large adults and their daughter also climbed in. I was freaked out, thinking our car exceeded the safe weight limit. I was certain we were overloaded and sure to crash. But we didn't. I suspect the daughter thought I was weird, however, because I never looked out at the views, but kept my eyes on the floor.

Tina and Percell took a shore excursion to Oia, a stunning cliffside city on the northern tip of the island. Tina says she's never seen anything to equal its beauty.

We talk about our families and our lives. Turns out Percell is the only boy in his family for several generations, so he was spoiled.

When he says he was spoiled rotten, Tina raises her eyebrows and nods in agreement. And we all laugh.

He says when he was a kid, he loved eggs. His mom had a rule that you could eat only two eggs at a meal. So after his two-egg meal at home, he'd go over to his grandma's and get two more.

When his mother found out what was happening, she confronted her mother about it. Her mother said, "Don't say a thing to me about giving Percell all the eggs he wants. When you were a little girl, you loved chocolate, and I gave you all the chocolate you wanted."

Percell smiles and adds, "That solved the problem."

He talks about his volunteer work in prisons. For years, Al did volunteer work in the prisons, so the two of them start comparing notes, while Tina and I talk about how much we love Greek food. And how concerned we are about our aging parents.

Following breakfast, Al and I spend the morning on our balcony, breathing in the fresh, warm Mediterranean air as our ship floats by forest-green islands.

He's reading his fifth or sixth thriller, and I'm writing notes about this trip. Such a lovely morning.

At noon, we go ashore.

Argostoli is a quiet little town on the island of Cephalonia. We find a cafe with free Wi-Fi and decide to take a long lunch there. Al orders a Greek meat pie. I have a big Greek salad – chunks of delicious tomato, cucumber, feta cheese, olives and red onion.

The smells of cigarette smoke and fried fish blend with the aroma of coffee and fresh veggies.

We eat on a covered but open-sided porch, with the ocean breeze wafting through. Many of the others eating lunch here are Skyping with folks back home.

I find it so amazing that we can be on the other side of the world and still maintain nearly instant contact with friends and family back home.

Paul Simon's 1986 album "Graceland" has a song called "The Boy in the Bubble." It's about war and destruction, but strangely, some of the lyrics flow through my mind as I watch Al email, and other people Skype. The words say we're living in the time of miracles and wonders, from the long-distance call to the ever-present camera following us all.

I've certainly seen these technological wonders during this trip.

On the street that runs in front of the cafe, a little train with many tourist-stuffed cars drives by. We considered buying at ticket for this "scenic" ride, but thought we'd rather spend our money on lunch and our time on email.

Greek music plays in the background as we read messages from family and friends, and Al sends replies.

Then we order coffee and split a piece of home-made baklava. Delicious and more moderately sized than yesterday's.

Eventually, we leave our lovely table and wander the town, taking pictures as we go. A shuttered window. An ancient, weathered doorway. A brilliant red flower.

Strangely, we see no one but folks from our cruise ship. And there aren't many of them. There are museums here and a lighthouse and other sites, but we're happy just wandering around with our cameras. We enjoy our quiet stroll through the town and back to the ship.

By 6 p.m., our ship pulls up anchor and heads toward Venice.

One thing I must emphasize about this cruise – the food is fantastic: delicious, nutritious, beautifully presented, just wonderful in every way.

Tonight, for dinner, Al has veal and mashed potatoes. I have an eggplant and mushroom concoction with polenta and a flavorful tomato sauce along with cooked spinach. So delicious!

Tomorrow is a day at sea. It should be nice and restful in preparation for our afternoon and evening in Venice on Tuesday.

Monday, Oct. 13

AT SEA

Sunrises and sunsets are among the most beautiful times of day on a cruise.

After Al returns from morning Mass, we head to the dining room for breakfast.

He has waffles. They arrive with a little white vat of syrup, a little white vat of strawberry compote and a little white vat of whipped cream.

"What makes these exceptional," he says after a couple of bites, "is that the compote is made with fresh, delicious strawberries, not something from a jar."

I'm enjoying an egg-white frittata with sun-dried tomatoes and low fat cream cheese and a bowl of muesli topped with fresh berries.

BEHIND-THE-SCENES KITCHEN TOUR

We love sea days because they offer opportunity for rest and reflection. Sea days also give us the chance to do interesting things onboard such as taking classes, going to an art auction, attending lectures or going on a behind-the-scenes tour.

Today I'm taking a behind-the-scenes kitchen tour. Al passes, preferring to read.

The tour starts at 10:30 a.m. in the coffee pantry, where java is brewed. The pantry is strategically close to the dining room so that the morning brew arrives at the table fresh and hot.

The fragrance of brewing coffee surrounds us as we continue our tour.

Next, comes the dishwashing area, where glasses, silverware, china, trays and plate covers are washed. Separate machines handle glassware and chinaware. China and cutlery are prewashed by hand before being fed into the dishwashing machines.

Pots and pans are washed elsewhere.

The cold kitchen is where cold appetizers, cheese platters and sandwiches are made and all salads are prepared. As we shuffle through, chefs energetically chop cabbage (red and green) and carrots. Their knives are so much sharper than the knives back in my California kitchen!

Our guide points out eight floor-to-ceiling cabinets filled with shelves for cold appetizers. As we head out of the cold kitchen, we're offered samples of cheese – little yellow and white squares, each with a toothpick for easy handling.

Next, we enter the hot kitchen, where warm dishes like omelets, pancakes, waffles and appetizers, soups and entrees are prepared.

Here we watch cooks making sauces, while others stir soups. The mix of fragrance makes my mouth water.

At this tour stop, we sample various sausages. Their fat little coin-shaped spheres have toothpicks in the middle for convenient handling.

Then we move past the tall roasting oven.

Our guide emphasizes that all dishes are prepared in small batches to maintain the best taste, texture and temperature of the food.

The last tour stop is the pastry shop. Al would be in heaven here. He'd probably never leave. I'd have to put out an all-points bulletin: Missing Person – Sweetheart with sweet tooth.

In the pastry shop, the chef and his six assistants prepare desserts, pies, cookies, chocolates, petites fours, and more. We pause to watch a chef create little frogs and turtles out of almond paste and chocolate. He's a food artist, making darling and delicious characters almost too precious to eat.

The entire kitchen area from one end to the other is stainless steel and we're told it's cleaned thoroughly four times a day.

As our tour ends, we're offered fresh-baked cookies. A sweet ending to a fascinating look behind the scenes.

This tour did not include the bread bakery, butcher shop, fish preparation area or the fruits and vegetable preparation and storerooms. Those areas exist on other decks.

But our guide points out that the baker and his staff prepare more than 20 different kinds of bread. Each day they bake 140 loaves of bread, 120 loaves of French bread, 5,000 dinner rolls, 1,000 croissants and 1,000 Danish pastries.

"We even bake our own hamburger buns and frankfurter rolls," he says.

Our tour information sheet lists the average weekly consumption of food on board the Nieuw Amsterdam. Here is what it says:

* meat and meat products	11,830 pounds
* poultry	3,814 pounds
* fish	1,875 pounds
* seafood	2,575 pounds
* butter & margarine	1,675 pounds
* fresh vegetables	137,500 pounds

* potatoes	7,750 pounds
* water melon	2,300 pounds
* dairy	5,500 quarts
* ice cream	300 gallons
* eggs	23,040
* sugar	950 pounds
* flour	3,500 pounds
* assorted sodas	362 cases
* assorted beers	332 cases
* Champagnes & sparkling wines	450 bottles
* assorted wines	1, 636 bottles
* water	280 cases

✺✺

After lunch, Al and I laze around on our balcony. Al reads, I write, and sometimes we do nothing but watch the ocean. I find it luxurious to have long stretches of free time. Love the fact that I can simply stare at the ocean or the sky for as long as I want. I feel so free when I have nothing I must do ... or when I have nothing at all to do.

I realize that some people find stretches of unscheduled time boring, but I don't.

After a while, I decide to go check out some of the onboard art, but discover that my room key is missing. I'd slipped it into my shoe for the kitchen tour (because I had no pockets in the slacks I wore, and I didn't want to carry a purse), but the key is no longer in my shoe.

"How stupid is this," I say irritably. "I've lost my room key."

"Just tell them at the front desk," Al says. "No big deal. Take mine, I'm just going to be here reading until you get back."

"But if I take your key, you'll have no lights," I say, reminding him that the key in the slot by the door keeps the electricity on in our cabin.

"Just go. You don't need a key. I'll be here when you get back."

At the front desk, I somewhat sheepishly explain the situation.

The man behind the counter smiles and says, "No problem. I'll make you another."

With a few strokes on his computer keyboard, he promptly cancels my old key and with a few more strokes, makes me a new one.

"How many people lose their room keys on a cruise like this?" I ask.

He laughs and says, "About 200."

Suddenly I don't feel quite so stupid.

✿✿

At 3 p.m. Al and I head for royal Dutch high tea in the main dining room. Every day of this cruise, high tea has been served at 3 p.m., but we've been too busy to attend. Today, we indulge in this rather genteel ritual.

Upon entering the dining room, each of us is handed a white china plate about the size of a generous salad plate. We then walk along a serving counter filled with beautiful and richly decorated desserts – chocolate-covered strawberries, apple cupcakes, cookies dusted with powdered sugar, baked chocolate goods, custardy squares, lemon squares and other delicacies – an almost endless array of baked and fruity goods. Way too many to try.

We carry our plates – now mountainous with desserts – to a table where we sit with others. They're all eyeing their tasty treasures.

Waiters in white jackets and gloves and carrying silver trays bring us tea. We each get a cup and saucer, a small teapot with boiling water, and a tea bag of the flavor of our choice. I have herbal lemon. Al has chamomile.

The small talk at our table is small indeed. And totally unmemorable. We're all focused on the goodies and only the goodies.

After tea, I decide to do laundry. Some cruise ships have laundromats on board. This one does not. All cruise ships offer laundry and dry-cleaning services, but I find the cost excessive, so I begin to wash our underwear in the tub.

As I suds and rinse and suds and rinse, I think of all the women around the world washing clothes in rivers. All the generations of women who have washed clothes by hand. I think of my own mother who, when I was a toddler, did the washing in a machine that had rollers to squeeze out the sudsy water. And rinsing tubs, to make sure the soap was totally out of the clothing before it was hung on the line.

As I hand-wash our undies, I feel at one with the ancient history of women doing laundry. But the romantic connection is short-lived.

Washing clothes by hand is work. Even on a cruise! Soon I'm sweating and wondering if I'm really getting our clothes clean. When I'm finished, I realize I don't have the strength to squeeze out all the water.

So I enlist Al's larger hands and bigger biceps. "Just squeeze each thing until it's almost dry," I instruct.

I can tell he's amused. But his amusement, like my washing, is short-lived. Squeezing out the water is fun only for the first two or three items. Then it's work.

Eventually we finish our task, and using hangers from the closet and the back of our balcony chairs, I spread out our stuff, and hope it will dry by bedtime.

There's a clothesline in the bathroom, but I like the idea of the sea breeze and sunshine drying our clothes.

Tomorrow we'll be back in Venice with clean undies, ready for the next phase of our European adventure.

Tuesday, Oct. 14

BACK IN VENICE

Gondolas are always at the ready near St. Mark's Square.

As it has from the beginning, the sun is shining when we awaken to our last day of the cruise. I can't believe that we're almost finished. We're supposed to dock at Venice this afternoon. We'll sleep on board tonight and then depart in the morning. This fabulous cruise ends after breakfast tomorrow.

In the lido, we see Tina and Percell, and the four of us stake a table next to the windows. The whole place is buzzing. Everyone, it seems, is excited to be nearing Venice. After eating hearty breakfasts and refilling our coffee cups, we sit and visit.

Our talk is all about our aging parents. Percell's mother died with Alzheimers. Tina's mother is 90 and beginning to suffer dementia. Al's parents are both deceased. My mother has passed on, and my 95-year-old father suffers from Lewy body disease.

When we were young, our challenges had to do with our futures – could we make it through college? Could we find a good job with a good income? Could we afford the kind of house we want? Could we find a good mate? Were we fulfilling our potential?

Now our challenges rotate around health issues and death. What can you say, other than "The circle of life."

But we can't linger long over such serious subjects, when we've got Venice to look forward to.

Before we part, we exchange email addresses and promise to keep in touch.

✳✳

Since I've been to Venice twice before, I know what I want to share with Al this afternoon. He had fun introducing me to Amsterdam. I'll have fun introducing him to St. Mark's Square.

Venice is as much an idea or an experience as a place. At least for me. The idea I carry in my heart includes beauty, history, romance, culture, as well as decline and decay and deterioration. The sea, which served to protect the refugees who founded Venice, now threatens to destroy this mystical city of water and light.

In 1987, UNESCO named Venice a World Heritage site. The entire city, with the Grand Canal slicing through it, is a world heritage site. And rightly so. From the winged lion of St. Mark, to the bobbing black gondolas, to the marble arch of the Rialto Bridge, Venice is a place to be savored. And we plan to take our time and do our savoring together this afternoon.

✹✹

As soon as we dock, Al and I (and scores of others) leave the ship. Because we missed our chance at the start of our cruise to ride down the Grand Canal, I'm determined that we do it now.

We head for the People Mover. This driverless, elevated tram near the cruise ship terminal, takes us to Piazzale Roma near the train station. It is not expensive but there are lots of steps to climb to get up to the tram and back down to the street.

At the railway station, we board a vaporetto (water bus) and head down the Grand Canal. Our goal: St. Mark's Square, the heart of Venice, roughly two miles away.

Our ride is like cruising through a painting. A living painting. The choppy water splashes as we chug along. Gorgeous palaces line either side. Some look in desperate need of repair. Boats of all kinds fill the canal itself – buses like ours, small motor boats, gondolas, work boats hauling cargo, and yachts.

Our vaporetto is stuffed full. There aren't enough seats for everyone, so many of us cling to poles and sway with the movement of the bus. The canal is as noisy as a New York City street, with boats honking and the water splashing. Al and I snap photo after photo with our digital pocket cameras. We've lost all objective control: everything is beautiful and we snap away, trying to capture it all.

As we pass under the Rialto Bridge, we remind ourselves that we have a room near here for tomorrow night. The area is bustling. It will be fun to explore on foot.

Our ride down the Grand Canal takes a good 40 minutes. During the entire ride, we barely dare to blink, lest we miss some of the glowing beauty of this broad, historic thoroughfare.

When we finally scramble off, near Piazza San Marco, we're enfolded in a multitude. Looks like everyone has the same idea.

The vaporetto station is close to two tall 12th-century columns that stand between St. Mark's Square and St. Mark's Basin. High atop one sits Mark's winged lion. The other holds St. Theodore battling a crocodile. But to reach them and the Doge's Palace, we must walk a broad bayside sidewalk. Swarming with tourists like us, this walkway feels very narrow.

Artists have set up their store/studio arrangements along this walkway, displaying paintings, drawings and photos. Most of the artists are actually working at easels or tables. The smell of oil paints swirls with the salty odor of the bay and the smell of sweaty humans. The painters are painting, the pastel artists are drawing, and all are eager to have us stop and look at their work. Every picture is beautiful. We dare not pause.

The artists and their works line the bayside of the walkway. On the other side stretches a line of booths selling postcards and souvenirs, gelato and other tourist-type goodies.

We push along, passing these busy business people, and next we come to a large Gondola dock, where many slim, black, graceful boats and their gondoliers wait for passengers.

Eventually, we reach the two columns, between which executions once took place. The Doge's Palace stands nearby. But before we turn left and wander along the front of the palace to the actual

St. Mark"s Square, I want Al to see the elegant Bridge of Sighs.

So, while most of the crowd turns left, we continue along the basin side of the palace until we reach the next corner (and the narrow canal running along the back of the palace).

The stone bridge spanning this slim canal is Ponte della Paglia (the Bridge of Straw). It is so named because this is where the bales of straw were unloaded for the Doge's Palace and the prison.

Standing on the Bridge of Straw with our back to the basin, we can see the enclosed Bridge of Sighs, high above the canal, connecting two wings of the palace.

Convicted prisoners walked this bridge from the palace to the prison. Its two small, barred windows allowed convicts one last look at the beautiful city and its turquoise bay, before being locked away.

Years ago, when I was here, I took the palace tour and walked the Bridge of Sighs and gazed out those tiny windows and imagined how painful it must have been for the prisoners to realize they would not be seeing their city for years.

Here's a fact I find interesting: The architect of the Bridge of Sighs, Antonio Contino, was the nephew of the Swiss engineer who built the Rialto Bridge, Antonio da Ponte.

Because of the numerous stairs and miles of walking required for the Doge's Palace tour, Al and I will not take it. But we have a blast photographing the sculptures adorning the palace exterior and snapping pictures of the gondola floating beneath the Bridge of Sighs.

By the time we retrace our steps, turn at the columns and head for St. Mark's Basilica, the crowds have thinned out. I remember the huge, squat, domed basilica and the massive crowds trying to enter it, and am happily surprised when we reach the entrance to find barely a line ahead of us.

There is no charge for entering the basilica. The first time I was in Venice, basilica crowds were so thick, I was physically squeezed between those ahead of me and those behind. I felt like a sardine clasped in a great river, with no ability to do anything except go with the flow.

But today is completely different. In just minutes, we're inside, awed and quieted by its perpetual interior twilight. There is plenty of space and time, and we oooh and ahhh and stare. Built in the 11th century, the basilica combines Byzantine and Western styles with its Byzantine domes and French Gothic spires. Its layout follows the Greek cross design. The place is crowned by a bulbous dome flanked by four smaller domes, and the five entrances are all arched.

Like Istanbul's Blue Mosque, the interior space is immense. Glittering mosaics cover all the overhead domes – gold everywhere.

Biblical scenes and lighted candles and colored marble columns, emeralds and pearls and people praying in the pews. Consecrated in 1094, this is Venice's holiest shrine.

Since A.D. 830, the bones of St. Mark have rested beneath the high altar. Evidently, St. Mark's remains were stolen in 828 from their tomb in Alexandria, Egypt. The story is that the thieves covered the saint's mummified corpse with pickled pork, to keep curious Muslims away. Imagine that.

We sit in one of the chapels — dozens of slim, white candles burning at one side — and just let the size and silence sink in. Of course, it isn't really silent. People whisper and there's the sound of feet shuffling on marble, but the sounds are background soft.

Eventually, we walk back out into the sunny square, and head for the Campanile (the 325-foot-tall bell tower). We'll ride the elevator to the top of Venice's tallest structure, and see the city from the sky. Tickets for the ride are eight euros. The line is a little longer than at the basilica, but we don't wait more than 15 minutes.

It is well after 3 p.m. when we step from the elevator onto what I'll call the observation level. There's quite a crowd here, but everyone's polite, sharing space at the large, open windows on the four sides of the tower. Protective fencing covers the windows, but there's plenty of room for hand-held cameras to poke through and get glorious shots of the city, its canals and the many islands surrounding Venice.

The stunning views, brilliant in the afternoon sunlight, are intoxicating. We don't want to turn away, so Al and I make our way around from window to window, twice, aiming our cameras at the endless expanse of red-tiled roofs, punctuated by church spires.

Al also photographs the huge bells above our heads. They're at least three feet in diameter, and their clappers look like baseball bats. I don't want to be here when they ring. I suspect these bells inflict instant (if temporary) deafness on anyone here in the tower when they peal the hour.

Sated with beauty and wonder, we ride the elevator back down to the square, buy a bottle of water from one of the many vendor booths and find a bench to rest on.

Al thinks the square is crowded, but this is nothing compared with what it was when I was here before. Back then, I'd have been lucky to find six inches to lean against anywhere, and here we've found actual sitting space on a bench.

Back then, the place was full of dark gray pigeons, and so many people I could barely breathe. This afternoon, there are far fewer pigeons, and the crowds are thin enough to allow a real feel for this huge and beautiful square.

Refreshed, we decide to wander over to the Clock Tower, and explore the street beneath it.

Built during the Renaissance in 1496, the clock tower marks the entry to a shopping street, and we wonder what we can find on that street. Leaving the square behind, we duck through the arched gate and are immediately engulfed with a shopping throng. Windows of jewelry, purses, masks and more line the crowded cobblestone street. When we come upon a gelato shop, we know precisely what to spend our money on.

And later, when we've had enough of the shoppers, we wander back to Piazza San Marco and simply enjoy the scene. No sound of auto or Vespa fills the air. With exquisite colonnades lining three sides of the plaza, I feel like I'm in a lacey fairy tale.

A quote from Truman Capote comes to mind: "Venice is like eating an entire box of chocolate liqueurs in one go."

✵✵

Back on board, we're hungry, but the lido is closed and so are the dining rooms. Then we remember a fast-food place not far from the lido deck swimming pool. I'm not a fan of fast food, but we're "starving." I have to put quotes around that word, and you know why. No one on this cruise is anywhere near starving. Nonetheless, Al and I are hungry and want to eat now.

So off we go to the Dive In, where hamburgers and hot dogs and French fries are always available.

Al scarfs down a hot dog. I get a grilled chicken sandwich. The food hits the spot.

After our repast, what else but a nap.

VENICE ON FOOT

One of the many ornate street lamps in Venice.

For this, the final night of our cruise, we decide to scout out the bed and breakfast where we've reserved a room for tomorrow. It's near the Rialto Bridge in the Jewish ghetto part of town, and once we find it, we can grab a vaporetto and return to St. Mark's Square to enjoy the nighttime orchestras.

We reason that by finding the place today, we'll save time in the morning getting settled there, and thus enjoy a long day of exploration with our cameras.

I scribble the address on a piece of paper, and slip it in my pocket. I'm happy we'll be staying in this historic part of Venice, just a block or so away from the oldest bridge spanning the Grand Canal.

We plan to catch a vaporetto at the train station to take us to the Rialto, but before we reach the station, we notice a yellow sign on the corner of a building, with an arrow pointing down a narrow street. The sign reads "Rialto." And on a whim, we decide to walk to the bridge. Venice is small. How far can it be?

The sun hangs low, a golden sphere, when we start off. The weather has been perfect on this trip and this evening is no exception. Warm, friendly air surrounds us. The narrow canal we cross, then recross, glows with golden light. Following the "Rialto" signs, we turn right, then left, then right and so on.

Over little bridges, across quiet canals, through streets so narrow only one person at a time can pass, around corner after corner we go.

"Where are we?" I ask, feeling like we're going in circles. Mine is a common question, since my sense of direction has always been poor. My Sweetheart, however, knows exactly where we are at any given moment.

But this evening he does not answer with quite his usual confidence. "We're headed for the bridge," he says.

We walk beside centuries-old stone buildings and along quiet, darkening canals lined with boats moored for the night.

As shadows darken the waterways, lights blink on in shops and restaurants.

After a while, my knees and feet start to hurt. I can imagine how Al's knees must feel, but he doesn't complain.

This is a much longer walk than I expected.

One reason Venice is so other-worldly is that there are no cars, buses, Vespas or other motor vehicles on its streets. No wheeled vehicles at all. Why? Because, every few feet there's a bridge. Four-hundred bridges in the city I'm told – among them, the Bridge of Breasts, the Bridge of Fists, the Bridge of the Barefoot, the Bridge of Courtesy, the Bridge of Humility, the Bridge of Paradise and so on and so on. Four hundred bridges and 2,000 alleyways.

And by now, I'm pretty sure we've crossed half the bridges and wandered most of the jigsaw alleys.

I read somewhere that Goethe said that in a typical Venitian street you can touch both sides by putting your hands on your hips. And he was telling the truth.

We turn more corners, walk streets lined with shops selling jewelry, clothing, artwork, handmade paper. We pass restaurants filled with diners raising wineglasses above flickering candles.

"Where are we?" I ask, not expecting an answer.

The streets grow dark.

We turn more corners, always following the (now illuminated) yellow signs pointing to "Rialto" and find ourselves in narrow, deserted alleyways. No stores here and no canals. It feels a little scary with no one else around. But the shore excursion lecture said there are few serious crimes committed in Venice, and I cling to that assurance.

A few more turns and twists and we're back among shoppers. Crowds of youth talking and giggling and snapping pictures with their phones. I ask a teenage girl, "Is Rialto this way?"

"Yes. Yes." She says enthusiastically. "About 15 more." And then she's off with her cloud of chattering friends.

And I'm wondering, 15 more what? Minutes? Miles?

"This is no fun," I say to Al. "No fun at all."

He says, "We'll soon be there."

"Ha!" I say. "How do you know?"

"Because that young girl just told us. Only 15 more." And we both start laughing.

If only we were near the Grand Canal we could hop on a vaporetto. But we're in the middle of a darkened, crooked and unpredictable fairly land maze of stone buildings and streets.

"We're lost," I say.

"But we're lost in Venice," he says, voice glowing. "Is there any better place on earth to be lost?"

As we climb a high, large bridge clasped in the full blackness of night, my energy gives out. "I'm done," I say, leaning against the stone railing, trying to catch my breath. "I want to go home and soak my feet."

Al leans against the railing, also breathing heavily.

"We don't have much farther to go," he says, although his voice lacks firm conviction.

As we gaze down the dark, calm watery path beneath our bridge, we see tremulous reflections of lights from nearby homes. A whole line of gently flickering points of light floating and rippling along the dark, mysterious canal. The sight draws us together in a long and comforting embrace.

We're in an incredibly beautiful place. And we're here together, enveloped by a darkness that feels contented and comfortable. I wouldn't be surprised if a Baroque quartet began to play. This whole journey seems enchanted. But then my feet remind me that they aren't the least bit happy.

We continue our trek ... walking hand in hand, turning, crossing bridges, turning, trudging, turning again, and suddenly, there it is: the elegant arched marble Rialto Bridge rising 24 feet above the Grand Canal, ablaze with lights and alive with crowds.

Vaporetti pull up and depart every few minutes. Knots of shoppers, carrying bags, climb and descend the bridge that has stood here since 1591. Canalside restaurants sparkle and hum with diners. The clink of wineglasses and the babble of voices fill the nighttime air.

The place is dazzling.

"We did it," Al says, slipping his arm around my waist and drawing me close. "I think we walked halfway across Venice."

What a way to end our cruise!

AL'S THOUGHTS ABOUT THIS TRIP
(Written March 28, 2015)

*V*enice. *The Eagle has landed, or at least the Nieuw Amsterdam has docked. The end of our voyage.*

Sixteen all-too-short days: 7,800 land and sea miles; nine hours time-shifted from that abrupt iPad wakeup (crickets) in our California home. Three new countries on my "been there" list (Italy, Greece, Turkey): two for Sunny who'd never seen the Netherlands or Turkey.

Tens of thousands of calories eaten; thousands of photos taken; what felt like (still feels like) scores of miles on old knees. And old hips, too.

Lots of statistics, lots of memories, lots of beauty and wonder and, yes, amazement. Not bad for an old guy. And I'm – we're – still going. Miles and promises before we sleep. More amazement to come, I'm sure.

A trip like this forces one to rethink longstanding beliefs. Take the concept of "old," for a starter.

As mentioned earlier, I've always thought of "old" as Gold Rush times – 1849ish. (Some Californians think of "old" as "last week," but that's another story).

On this trip, however, we've seen houses and churches built when Massachusetts was occupied solely by native peoples. Houses that are not just still standing but are in daily use. And those buildings are new construction when compared to what we've seen in Greece and Turkey. My definition of "old" has been forever changed.

It's not just buildings, though: it's my broader sense of the continuum of human experience: the sweep of history, if I may.

I'm something of a history buff, but nothing I've read is the same as walking the very road that Anthony and Cleopatra walked.

To stand in the very garden where Jesus' mother spent her last days; to sail down a waterway exactly as a sultan once did; to be in places where the course of nations was forever altered; these are the things that stand out for me. Book-history will never be quite the same for me.

And people. This trip was a unique opportunity to see the commonality of humankind. The women wrapped in black burkas, only their eyes showing, playing with their children; the pomegranate juice seller, a small businessman looking to make a sale; the young *people, huddled over their coffee, talking animatedly in languages I don't understand; the refugees, looking for new homes; yes, even the sex workers, coyly showing their wares. None different, really than you and me and our neighbors.*

This trip made real for me how much we all have in common, culture and language and other differences notwithstanding. In an era of deep polarization, this is good to see. I needed it.

Sunny often asks me, "Are you having fun?"

The answer, as any married man knows, is "Of course." But, truthfully, this has been a fun trip. I've loved the baklava and the sunsets (and rises) and the sights and the smells. And the gelato (more to come on gelato, I'm sure).

I've been delighted to discover that this old body can do more and go farther than I thought it could, to great reward.

If you, dear reader, wonder whether you dare travel to some long-dreamed-of place, my answer is: give it a shot. You may well be astounded.

SUNNY'S PARTING THOUGHTS

I simply loved this trip. Despite the rotten flight to Amsterdam, everything about this trip was special. But for me that's how travel is.

Travel helps me climb out of the "every day," and explore new places, learn new things, eat new and different foods and just have fun. Travel is challenging and at the same time refreshing. Even renewing.

As science fiction author Ray Bradbury points out, "Half the fun of travel is the aesthetic of lostness."

And Al and I certainly experienced that aesthetic. It has given us a very good story to share, thus enriching us and our journey.

If you've been dreaming about something – taking a trip or learning a skill or earning a long-dreamed-of college degree – I encourage you to do it. Now. While you can. You'll not only know the joy of fulfilling that desire, you'll enrich your existence and make lifelong memories.

Now here's some background on our trip and a glimpse of our future publishing plans:

When Sweetheart Al signed us up for a 12-day Mediterranean cruise, little did we know our trip would morph into 42 days of exciting travel. But it did. Here's how.

We added four days on at the start, reasoning it would help us recover from jet lag before the cruise. That's how we added Amsterdam.

Then I got to thinking about coming back home after the cruise. I don't like flying (have I mentioned that before?) I thought it would be a horrible ending to a wonderful trip, if we left the ship only to climb on a plane and fly for hours to get home.

So I searched the Internet to see if I could find a repositioning cruise that would take us from Europe to the USA. I'd much rather float on water, than be in a jet roaring through the skies while sitting in cramped and miserable seats cheek to jowl with who-knows what?

As you may know, repositioning cruises offer extremely affordable prices. A repositioning cruise is when a ship moves from one region at the end of the season (such as the Mediterranean during the summer cruise season) to another region (like the Caribbean for the winter cruising season).

I found a great repositioning cruise: 14 days from Barcelona to Miami for about the price of one transatlantic airplane coach ticket to San Francisco. I signed us up immediately.

Because I neglected to check our travel schedule in my haste to grab the excellent price, we ended up with 12 days between when we left our ship in Venice and when we were to climb on board in Barcelona.

So we spent those days exploring Venice, Florence, Rome and Barcelona.

And our trans-Atlantic cruise to Miami added another 14 days to our trip. Forty-two unforgettable days filled with discovery, relaxation and fun.

This trip took a great deal of planning, and included train travel, cruise ship travel and airplane travel, to say nothing of all we discovered while exploring on foot. We saw so much and did so much and had such a great time doing it all that one book about our trip would have been hundreds of pages long. Way too long for most readers!

So we've written three travel memoirs about it:

Cruising the Mediterranean

From luminous canals in Amsterdam and Venice to the stunning mosaics of Istanbul's Blue Mosque, this spirited travel memoir takes readers on the trip of a lifetime.

Finding Ourselves in Venice, Florence, Rome & Barcelona

Aging adventurers discover the power of place while exploring fascinating cities at their own relaxing pace.

Cruising the Atlantic

Our Epic Journey from Barcelona to Miami

You can find them, and our first travel memoir, **Cruising Panama's Canal** *Savoring 5,000 Nautical Miles and 500,000 Decadent Calories*, at Amazon.com.

We plan to continue traveling and writing about our travels for as long as our bodies allow.

Thank you for coming along with us on our unforgettable Mediterranean cruise.

ACKNOWLEDGEMENTS

Writing this book has been a lot of work. But it's been fun work. We liked sorting through our photographs and reminding ourselves of all we did, all we saw. All that surprised and delighted us.

It was fun choosing which aspects of our trip to share, which stories we think will most entertain or educate.

And even though it's tedious to write and rewrite and throw out and rework scenes and paragraphs and sentences in our attempt to capture the moments as they happened, and share the emotions as they rose and ebbed, we felt a stream of fun or fulfillment flowing through all that hard writing and rewriting labor.

Although it can be true that writing is a lonely art practiced in isolation, this book is the result of many helpful people to whom we are indebted.

There are my inspiring writer friends who continue to encourage our efforts. Members of Writers

Unlimited in Calaveras County, California, and members of the Redwood Writers Club in Sonoma County, California, have been an unending source of help and useful criticism.

And there are others without whose help this book may never have come into being.

Developmental editor Elaine Silver read portions of our manuscript in its early stages and gave us excellent suggestions for improvement.

Tina Johnson, a friend we met on this cruise and a former editor at Redbook Magazine, read an early draft and gave us encouraging feedback. She also took our author bio photograph. It was taken on our afternoon in Athens when the four of us — Al and I and she and her husband, Percell, — ducked into a cafe to escape an afternoon downpour.

Carl Sommers, a retired New York Times editor, polished our sentences until they shone. His meticulous expertise with grammar and punctuation along with his probing questions helped us improve many a passage.

Parker Wallman created our exquisite cover, and offered other design suggestions. Working with him has been a pleasure. Parker's vision, enthusiasm, artistry and focus are unmatched. And to top that off, he lives just down the road a piece in our new home state of North Carolina. How cool is that!

And, as always, we must thank you, dear reader, for you are the reason we've written this book. Without you, we'd have little motivation to write about our travels.

AUTHOR REQUEST

If you enjoyed our book, please tell your friends about it. We appreciate when our readers spread the word online and in person. It's a great encouragement to us.

And if you have the time and are so inclined, we welcome reader reviews and ratings.

Just go to our book's page at Amazon.com to leave your comments and ratings. To reach our book's page, simply type the title in the Amazon search bar.

Thank you.

ABOUT THE AUTHORS

Al and Sunny Lockwood have traveled by foot, car, rail, air and cruise ship. They've camped in national parks, hiked mountain trails, photographed springtime flowers in Death Valley and wintry surf along the rugged beaches of Northern California.

They've watched July 4th fireworks over Lake Tahoe, explored the Taos Pueblo and ridden the Great Smoky Mountains Railroad through forests ablaze with autumn colors.

And everywhere they go, they capture unforgettable moments — Al with his camera and Sunny with her reporter's notebook. Their work has been published in magazines and newspapers. It has been recognized with awards from the National Federation of Press Women and the California Newspaper Publishers Association,

Their first travel memoir, **Cruising Panama's Canal**, was a finalist in the 2014 National Indie Excellence Awards.

This photograph was taken in an Athens coffee shop, when Al and Sunny ducked inside to escape a sudden downpour.

You can contact Al and Sunny at sunnyandallockwood@gmail.com

Made in the USA
Middletown, DE
23 March 2018